Do-It-Yourself

Includes online audio
& instructional video

BANJO

BY MIKE SCHMIDT

D0721498

PLAYBACK+
Speed • Pitch • Balance • Loop

To access audio and video visit:
www.halleonard.com/mylibrary

Enter Code
1727-0176-1487-6054

ISBN 978-1-7051-0763-8

HAL•LEONARD®

Visit Hal Leonard Online at
www.halleonard.com

Contact us:
Hal Leonard
7777 West Bluemound Road
Milwaukee, WI 53213
Email: info@halleonard.com

In Europe, contact:
Hal Leonard Europe Limited
42 Wigmore Street
Marylebone, London, W1U 2RN
Email: info@halleonardeurope.com

In Australia, contact:
Hal Leonard Australia Pty. Ltd.
4 Lentara Court
Cheltenham, Victoria, 3192 Australia
Email: info@halleonard.com.au

CONTENTS

Welcome

Welcome to the realm of the 5-string bluegrass banjo. I assume that if you've gone as far as making the decision to learn the banjo, you've already developed an interest, if not a love, for the music—and something about the banjo in particular has "lit the fire." If you want to become a good banjo player and a good musician, immerse yourself in the music. Listen to the old masters, the contemporary bands—everything you can get your hands on.

In this book, we will explain everything you need to know—starting with the basics of playing your first notes—and take you through some intermediate and even advanced playing techniques.

Ultimately, this music is meant to be played, not read. By this, I mean it's important to use your ear and depend on it as much as, if not more than, the written music. For the purposes of this book, the written music is necessary, but the skills you learn here will give you the foundation to be able to put tunes together based on what you hear. This is not to say that you should expect to hear everything. After all these years, I still find myself referring to tablature on occasion; but for the most part, you should start to identify picking patterns, chords, and melodies purely by hearing them.

The 5-string banjo is a wonderful instrument. It can be played at all levels—from beginner to highly advanced—and give pleasure to the player and audience alike. In addition, there is absolutely no way to play *sad* music on this instrument. Even lost-love tunes and murder ballads are upbeat and unusually cheerful when played on the banjo.

To begin, you will need the following materials:

- A 5-string banjo with good strings
- One thumb pick and two finger picks
  - › Several sets—they get lost, stepped on, etc.
- A straight-backed chair without armrests
- A device on which to play the audio and video files included with this book
- A music stand (optional, but helpful)
- A banjo capo
- This book!

There are a few things to keep in mind when starting any instrument. There will be times when you'll have fun and make lots of progress, and there will be times when you'll be frustrated. When the frustration comes, and it will, don't take it too hard. Learning happens in spurts. After you learn something, you need time to solidify it before you can learn or absorb more. The best thing to do at these times is to review something you already know well, or just take a break. I've found that sometimes a day off can help the solidification process.

Speaking of practice, your progress will go hand-in-hand with the amount of time spent practicing. I would never insist that anyone practice three hours a day, but if you're enthusiastic, it won't be hard to do at least an hour almost every day. This, of course, does not take into consideration others in the house who may have their own opinions on the amount of banjo they care to listen to on a given day. At any rate, the more you practice, the quicker you'll progress.

Something I always suggest to new players is to get a good, solid instrument stand (on some, the banjo hangs by the peghead and rests against the base, which is much more stable than the traditional guitar stand). Instead of packing the banjo back into its case when you're done practicing, try putting it on the stand next to the couch or your favorite chair. That way, it's in plain sight, easy to pick up, and you might just find yourself playing a whole lot more than if you just schedule a certain block of time every day for practice.

As you work on the early exercises in this book, you will essentially be forming muscle memory—also known as "habits." For example, you need to play a right-hand roll hundreds, maybe thousands, of times until you can do it without thinking. That's muscle memory. I find that if I can speak normally while playing something, that pretty much proves I've committed the playing to memory. For this reason, it's important to be very careful when first learning any particular concept. If you learn it incorrectly and form the incorrect habit, it can be quite a chore to change or re-learn it. This goes for rolls, chords—everything.

In addition, I mentioned earlier that you might skip a day here and there. This is fine, but try never to miss more than one or two days in a row, especially in the early stages. When you first learn something, repetition is a good way to remember it. When it's new to you, several days away can cause you to lose or forget most of it, and this is a setback.

> **Important Note:** The left and right hands will be referred to constantly in this book, with the assumption that you are playing right-handed. I will often refer to the picking hand and the fretting hand, but for our purposes, the right hand is the picking hand and the left is the fretting hand.
>
> Of course, there are many left-handed people. I know some who play on a left-handed instrument and others who simply learned to play right-handed. If you walk into a music store, hoping to try out a lefty banjo, you may be out of luck. While some stringed instruments can simply be re-strung and turned around, the 5-string banjo neck is not symmetrical, meaning that a left-handed instrument is often a custom build, and this can be expensive. For this reason, lots of left-handed people choose to play right-handed. If you've not played a stringed instrument before, you may find that neither hand has a preference, so it's fairly easy to teach either hand to do its part. In short, I suggest you consider learning to play right-handed; but if you don't, please keep the above note in mind.

The title *Do-It-Yourself Banjo* means you're giving yourself lessons, and a lesson should be only as much as you can process at one time. Learning—and mastering—the material in this book could be a project that takes a few years. There's definitely a lot of work to be done, but there's no reason to make it painful, right?

Factors of Good Playing

One of the exciting things about bluegrass music is the speed with which it is sometimes played. This can also be a source of frustration for the beginner. Every student I've ever had (including myself) wanted to play fast, just like the records. There are several factors involved before you can speed things up. In order, they are:

1. **Accuracy.** This is most important. It is critical that you play as accurately as possible. If this means you need to stop and think before you hit the next note, that's fine. Playing the right notes is the first order of business.

2. **Smoothness.** After you play a pattern or song (or part of a song) enough to start forming muscle memory, you'll find you don't have to think too hard about the notes anymore. Here's where smoothness enters the picture. By smoothness, I mean an equal amount of time given to all notes. (Note: Of course, this refers to when you are playing patterns made up of the same type of notes, like quarter notes or eighth notes; we'll get more into this later.) It still doesn't have to be very fast—just smooth. Don't play anything faster than you can play it smoothly. Playing the easy parts quickly and then slowing down for the harder parts is not a good habit to get into.

3. **Speed.** Finally, after you have achieved accuracy and smoothness, you can begin to speed up the tune. As mentioned above, avoid the temptation to play the easy or familiar parts faster and the hard parts slower. Don't play any faster than the hardest part of the tune—you can't play any faster than your brain will let you. When those tricky parts get learned, you'll be able to play them faster. Then, you can speed everything up along with them. With systematic practice, you'll be playing faster—sooner.

I find that playing along with recordings is a great exercise, because they won't stop and wait for you. You have little choice but to try to keep up. If you make a mistake, ignore it and just keep going. With time, you'll see that you reuse certain licks and combinations. As you learn more licks, new songs will get up to speed sooner.

About the Audio and Video

Throughout the book, you will find symbols like the ones shown here. These are references to the audio and video recordings that come with this book. Featured on them are demonstrations of the techniques, methods, examples, and songs you will be learning. You can even play along with them.

In the front of the book, you will find a URL and a code number. This is your personal access to these files. Use your web browser to open the Hal Leonard My Library website (**www.halleonard.com/mylibrary**), enter your code, and you will have full access to listen to, view, and download the files.

My Library also includes the multi-functioned audio player PLAYBACK+, which allows you to slow down the audio tracks for this book without changing pitch *and* set loop points for difficult rolls or phrases you want to isolate for practice. This is a very useful tool for learning banjo!

On the audio recordings with this book, the banjo parts are deliberately played slower than they would normally be performed in a typical bluegrass setting. You may find they are still too fast to keep up with, and that's OK. It takes time and disciplined practice to reach that level of speed and skill, so you are encouraged to make use of the PLAYBACK+ slow-down and loop features.

Anatomy of the Banjo

Let's look at the 5-string banjo and its parts. Like most stringed instruments, the primary parts are the body, the neck, the peghead, and of course, the strings. The body creates the unique sound of the instrument; the neck allows you to choose the notes you wish to play; the peghead holds the pegs that tune the strings; and the strings are the source of the sound. There are other parts as well, and you can see them labeled in Figure 1. In the following sections, we'll look at some of these parts in more detail.

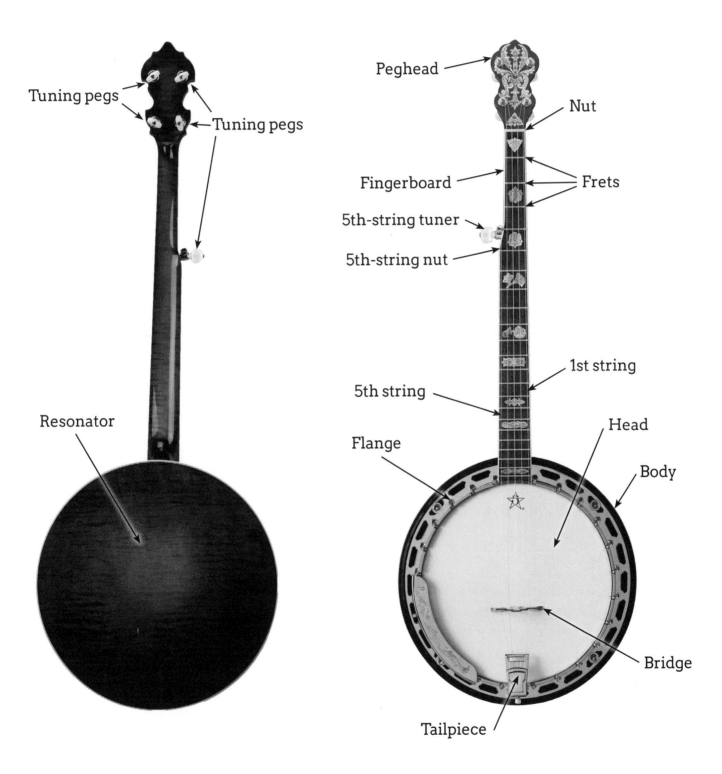

Fig. 1

Neck

Many of the techniques we will learn and use are centered around the *neck*. The neck is composed of several components, discussed here in their approximate order of importance.

Frets

Frets are the metal "dividers" placed on the fingerboard to delineate one note from another. On a standard 5-string banjo, there are 22 frets.

Fingerboard

The *fingerboard* is the flat wooden surface between the frets where the tips of the fingers press the string, holding it down across the frets and thus changing the pitch of the strings. There's physics at work here: If the vibrating length of the string is shortened or lengthened (which is what happens when you press the string down with your finger), the note produced will be higher or lower, respectively.

Bridge and Nut

These two parts serve similar purposes. They are the official end points of the strings. While the *bridge* isn't actually part of the neck, it is related. The parts of the strings that extend beyond the bridge and *nut* lead to anchor points and are not played (except for the occasional special effect or attempt at humor). The 5th string is shorter and has its own nut just before its tuning peg on the side of the neck.

Tuning Pegs

There are four *tuning pegs* on the peghead and one on the side of the neck. This is where the tension of the strings is adjusted to get the proper pitch for the *open* (unfretted) strings. The 5th and 1st strings have the same tension; however, because the 5th string is shorter, it sounds higher than the 1st string when played open—physics again.

Head

The *head* is the large, round surface of the body of the banjo. When the strings are picked, the head vibrates and resonates, amplifying the strings considerably. Most banjo heads are made of painted plastic, much like modern drum heads.

Tailpiece

The strings are anchored to the *tailpiece*, which holds them to the body of the banjo.

Resonator

The back of the body is called the *resonator*. The resonator acts as a sounding board, amplifying the sound produced by the strings and the head. It is held to the banjo by four or more screws or bolts that secure it to the flange. Usually, these bolts have knobs rather than screw heads, which allow you to tighten or loosen them with your bare hands.

Flange

The *flange* is a thin ring with baffles that connects the resonator to the pot (or body) assembly. The openings in the flange allow the sound from the resonator to be sent forward. Some banjos have no resonator and are noticeably quieter as a result. In bluegrass, it is typical to have a resonator (and a flange).

Holding the Banjo

When starting to learn banjo, the first things you need to work on are posture and hand position.

Posture

At first, it is probably best to practice in a sitting position. It is critical to have a nice straight chair—like a kitchen table chair or folding chair—with *no* arm rests. Arm rests should be avoided because they can get in the way of your arms, making free movement difficult. A chair that allows you to sit back a bit is all right; but if you lean back too much, it will be difficult to adapt to a comfortable standing posture when the time comes. See Figs. 2 and 3 for the right ways to sit and stand. Students that want to see the neck and strings better will tilt the banjo so it faces upward; this is especially bad for the fretting hand because the fingers are forced to reach much farther to do their job effectively. Generally, the body of the banjo should be flat against *your* body.

Fig. 2. Sitting Position

Fig. 3. Standing Position

When sitting, the round part of the banjo body should rest in your lap, between your legs. Don't try to balance it on one leg, because it will tend to roll off. Let both legs support it. Position it so the neck is approximately 45 degrees to the floor. Because the neck should be at this angle, I recommend using a strap, even when sitting! This will allow you to keep the neck in the correct position without having to hold it in place with the fretting hand.

Hands

Whether we're referring to the left hand or the right, we will be calling the fingers by their names. Some methods use numbers, but I think that's confusing; so, please have a look at Fig. 4. The best way to approach the banjo, as far as your hands are concerned, is to relax them both. Shake them loose, and they should relax into a position that might look as though you're holding a ball—wrists straight and fingers gently curved. If you find yourself holding the fingers rigidly—on either hand—stop and shake them loose, then continue.

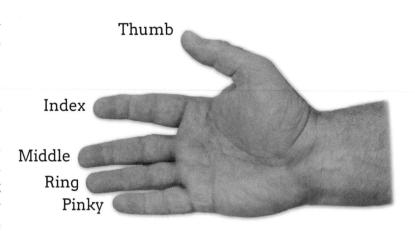

Fig. 4

Your left forearm should approach the neck from behind with a straight wrist. Your fingers should be relaxed and slightly curved so that the tips of the fingers touch the strings and fingerboard.

I cannot stress enough the importance of keeping the hand relaxed, not clenched. Be careful not to bend the wrist too much. Slight movement in the wrist is normal, but if you find your fingers or wrist at sharp angles, stop and shake them loose, then continue.

Finger Picks

The right hand is a bit easier to explain. First, you'll need to put on the picks. Typically, we use two metal finger picks for the index and middle fingers, and a plastic thumb pick... you know... for the thumb (see Fig. 5). There are metal thumb picks, but the thumb is a stronger digit, and the softer plastic balances the volume between the thumb and fingers.

Fig. 5. Finger Picks and Thumb Pick

The parts of the finger picks that slide onto the fingers can be bent slightly to make a good fit—not too tight, but enough to stay on. The tip part of the finger picks, the part that actually touches the strings, shouldn't be adjusted too much. The tips should extend about 1/8" beyond the tips of the fingers. The thumb pick should fit snugly on the top part of the thumb. If it is loose enough to slide past the first joint, it's too large. Try a smaller one.

When getting used to wearing and playing with picks, avoid the urge to play without them. Early on, it seems easier to play with bare fingers because you can feel what you're doing. That makes sense, but you won't get the necessary volume and tone, and playing *without* picks will not get you any more used to them. Also, many beginners—including myself—find that bending

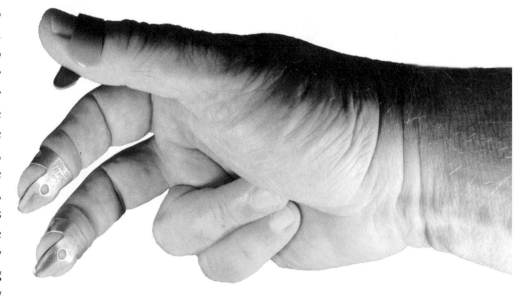

Fig. 6

the tips of the finger picks up and over the tips of the fingers makes it seem a bit more like playing without them. Again, volume and tone will suffer, along with accuracy, and you'll eventually find that leaving the picks in their original shape works best.

I'm not saying you shouldn't experiment; I'm merely trying to help you benefit from the experiences of others, including myself. Many actions or approaches may seem effective at first, but when more technique is learned, you'll find yourself needing to correct some bad habits.

Hand Position

It's time to get that picking hand in position. With the picks on, shake your hand loose as described earlier. Now, the picking hand must be "anchored" on the head of the banjo. Place the pinky in the corner created by the 1st string and the bridge (see Fig. 7). Although many sources say both the pinky and ring fingers must be planted here (as shown in the picture), I've never been able to keep the ring finger down and have had perfectly good results with only the pinky anchored. It's important to have at least one finger planted though, because it will help you to keep your position in relation to the strings. When you're picking at speeds near that of light, getting lost can be a serious problem, not to mention embarrassing. Trust me, I've been there.

Note that the closer you position the picks to the bridge, the brighter the sound you will get. You'll find that you might move around a bit depending on the sound or feel you're going for.

Fig. 7. Anchored Pinky and Ring Fingers

Tuning the Banjo

When the banjo is held in playing position, the lowest-positioned string—the string closest to the floor—is the 1st string. As we move upward, we count upward as well: 2nd, 3rd, 4th, and on top, the shorter 5th string. These are tuned to the following notes:

 Video 1

1st = D
2nd = B
3rd = G
4th = D
5th = G

Unlike most other stringed instruments, these are a little out of the usual order. The guitar and mandolin, for example, start with the highest pitch on the 1st string and go lower in pitch as you move through the string numbers. The 5-string banjo does this on strings 1 through 4, but then the 5th string jumps up to a high G. In the bluegrass style of playing, the 5th-string note is common to several chords and is used as a sort of drone string. As you're picking through a G chord, that high G note is part of the chord. It's also part of a C chord. It's not part of a D chord, but it sounds nice when played with the other notes of the D chord. Those three chords make up a lot of songs in a lot of musical styles. We will explore these chords in more detail later.

Tuning Methods

There are several ways to tune. Personally, I feel it is very important to train your ear so you can match your strings to those of another instrument, a keyboard, a pitch pipe, or tuning fork. There is also a variety of electronic tuners, and these are very handy in noisy environments. Over time, you will want to become comfortable with both your ear and a tuner. Whatever you use to tune, always keep picking the string as you adjust the tuning peg. If you turn the pegs without hearing it, you can't tell where you are; the string might get too high too fast and may even break.

To a Tuner

Electronic tuners are wonderful, and you can tune in almost any conditions. My only warning here is that you do not get too dependent on one. You need to develop your ear; and while it may take some time, your ear will improve. That said, there will be times when you just can't hear because of other noise or you may need to tune up quickly; those are the times when the electronic tuner is a great tool to have. They come in a variety of types, shapes, styles, and price ranges. Even the least expensive ones are accurate and easy to use. Check out Fig. 8 for an example. Like most, the tuner shown here is inexpensive, has a bright, easy-to-view dial, and comes in a variety of models that do a variety of things. The most common is the clip-on. It clips to your peghead and picks up the vibrations. Another variation of this is one that reads vibrations but also has a microphone, allowing you to use it for other instruments or voices.

Fig. 8. Electronic Clip-On Tuner

When you play a note, the tuner will recognize it and tell you whether it's accurate or not. In fact, if you aren't tuned to the right note, it will read that too. Say you're tuning the 1st string, which should be tuned to D. Maybe you're too low. The tuner will tell you it's a C. You need to get it up to D and then center the pointer so it's tuned exactly. A little to the left or minus (–) and you're *flat* (low); a little to the right or plus (+) and you're *sharp* (high). Do this for every string.

Watch Video 1 for the correct tuning notes. And remember, practice tuning to these notes with your ear; don't rely too heavily on the tuner.

To a Guitar

Three of the guitar's strings—2nd, 3rd, and 4th—are a direct match to the banjo. Ask your guitar player to pick the 2nd string (B) several times while you match your 2nd string to it. Do the same with the 3rd and 4th strings.

The 1st string is different. Your 1st-string note, D, does not appear as an open string on the guitar. So for your 1st string, ask the guitar player to play the 2nd string, 3rd fret.

Your 5th string is a higher G, so here, ask your guitar player to play the 1st string, 3rd fret.

By Ear

Tuning by ear requires that you hear the note you are tuning to, and that you hear it in the proper range. The easiest way to start might be to tune to another banjo. Use the video for this. Each open string is played several times so you can match yours to mine. This may be challenging at first, but with time, you will find it gets easier.

To Itself

If you have no other source to get the correct pitches, you can always tune the instrument to itself. It may not be perfectly in tune with the standard pitches, but it will sound fine as long as you're playing alone.

1. Start by getting the 4th string D close to what sounds correct.

2. Play the 4th string, 5th fret. This will be a G. Match the open 3rd string to this pitch.

3. Play the 3rd string, 4th fret. This will be a B. Match the open 2nd string to this pitch.

4. Play the 2nd string, 3rd fret. This will be a D. Match the open 1st string to this pitch.

5. Play the 1st string, 5th fret. This will be a high G. Match the open 5th string to this pitch.

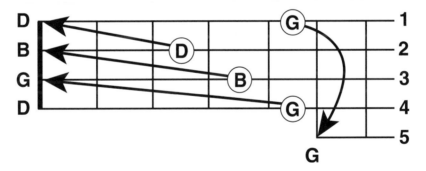

Fig. 9

To a Keyboard

If you have a piano or other keyboard available, you can tune to that, as well. I don't want to go too deeply into a piano lesson here, but if you know your notes on the keyboard or can find them with the help of Fig. 10, you can tune to the keyboard. The 1st string on the banjo is a D. There are several D notes on the piano. To find the correct one, we start by locating *middle C*. On a standard piano, this is literally the C key nearest the center of the keyboard.

Be careful if you're using an electronic keyboard. They can be set to play in any range, so the physical position of the middle C note may not necessarily play the correct note.

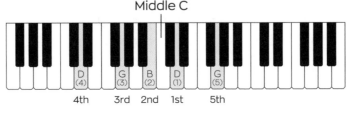

Fig. 10

Tablature

Anatomy of the Staff

Many stringed instruments use a form of written music called *tablature* (or *tab*). Like standard music notation, it appears on a *staff*. The banjo tab staff consists of five parallel lines, just like the standard notation staff; but this is a coincidence, because in tablature, each line represents a string, and this is a 5-string banjo. (Guitar tab, for example, has a six-line staff.)

At the far left of the staff in Fig. 11 is the word "tab" and a small set of numbers: 1 through 5. "Tab" indicates that you are, in fact, looking at tablature, and the small numbers tell you which lines represent which strings (these numbers, however, won't always be there). The top line of the tab staff represents the 1st string, the second line from the top is the 2nd string, and so on. When holding the banjo in playing position, the 1st string is positioned at the bottom (closest to the floor), which is the opposite of how it appears on the staff. Unlike standard notation, which uses note symbols to designate the pitches of notes on the staff, tab uses numbers on the lines to indicate finger positions on the neck.

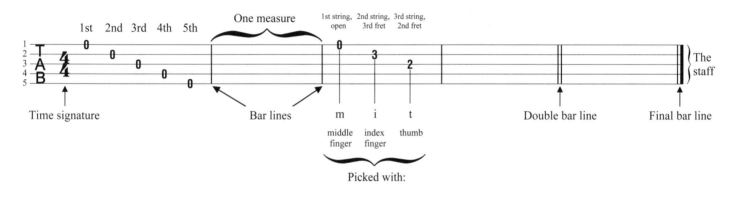

Fig. 11

The staff is divided into sections by vertical lines called *bar lines*. *Double bar lines* end a section or small example, while *final bar lines* end a song. The equally timed sections indicated by the bar lines are *measures*, or *bars*. A measure is a unit of time made up of *beats*, which are like the "pulse" of the music.

Time Signature

The *time signature* appears at the beginning of every piece of music and tells you two things:

1. How many beats there are in each measure
2. What type of note gets a single beat

The most common time signature is 4/4, shown in Fig. 11. (Note: Most banjo music is in *cut time*, which we will get to later.) The top number tells you that there are four beats per measure, and the bottom number tells you what type of note gets one beat. If we think of these as fractions, the bottom number, 4, can be thought of as a quarter (as in 1/4). So, the *quarter note* gets the beat, and there are four quarter notes (or the equivalent) per measure.

Quarter Note 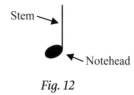 *Video 2*

Let's start with a standard quarter note (Fig. 12). It consists of an oval *notehead* and a straight *stem*. If a common measure consists of four beats, a quarter note is a quarter of that measure, or one beat.

Fig. 12

Now, let's look at one measure of standard notation, meaning "regular music." In Fig. 13, we see four quarter notes. When counting, we give each quarter note one beat. The notes shown here are all G. We count 1–2–3–4 evenly and play one note on each count. We restart each new measure at 1.

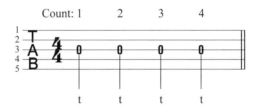

Fig. 13. Quarter Note—Standard Notation

Fig. 14 is exactly the same as Fig. 13, except it is written in tablature. Instead of the notehead, we use a number. In this example the number is zero (0). The quarter-note *value* (duration) is indicated by the straight stem. We have four quarter notes played *open* (zero fret) on the 3rd string, which is G.

Fig. 14. Quarter Note—Tablature

In these examples, the numbers above the notes indicate the beats. There are four beats in these measures. If we say the numbers 1–2–3–4, we would be playing one note on each count. Again, one quarter note = one beat. These numbers will not always be present in the written music.

Below each note in Fig. 14, we see the letter "t." This indicates that these notes are picked with the thumb. Soon, we will see the letters "i" and "m," indicating that the index and middle fingers will also be used.

Fig. 15 is a simple quarter-note exercise. We will count four beats in each measure and play a quarter note, picked with the thumb, on each beat. Notice in the last measure the curved lines connecting the notes to one another. These are *ties*. When two or more notes are tied together, you pick the first note and let it ring for the value of the picked note plus the tied notes. So, in the last measure you will pick the first note on beat 1 and let it ring through beats 2, 3, and 4.

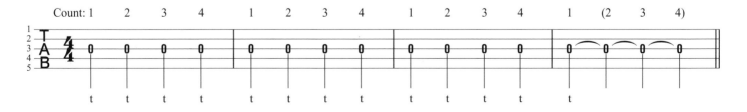

Fig. 15

Eighth Note

Taking this a step further, we have an *eighth note* (Fig. 16). Notice that the eighth note, in standard notation, consists of the oval notehead and straight stem—like a quarter note—but it also includes a curved *flag*.

Fig. 16

If we think in mathematical terms, two-eighths are equal to one-quarter: $2/8 = 1/4$. This means that two eighth notes can be played in the space of one quarter note. They're twice as fast.

With quarter notes, we count 1–2–3–4 and play a single quarter note on each beat. With eighth notes, we play two notes on each beat, so the note between each numbered beat is counted with an "and," or "&." The beats (1 through 4) do not change in speed; we just "sneak" the "ands" in between, playing eighth notes evenly on the numbered beats and the "ands." Commonly, musicians refer to the numbered beats as *downbeats* and the "ands" as *upbeats*.

When several eighth notes appear together, they may be written separately or connected. Fig. 17 shows one measure of individual eighth notes. Fig. 18 shows them grouped. We can replace the flags with a single bar (known as a *beam*), joining them in multiples of two, three, or four notes.

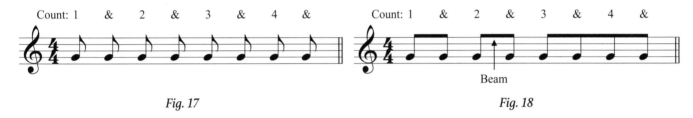

Fig. 17   *Fig. 18*

With all that in mind, eighth notes in tablature are written pretty much the same way, but instead of the oval noteheads, we use the numbers. So, the first measure of Fig. 19 shows four separated eighth notes and four eighth notes connected, or beamed together; they're played exactly the same way.

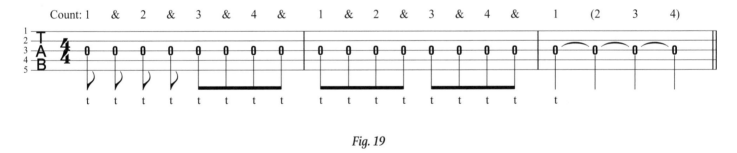

Fig. 19

Fig. 20 is a simple exercise combining quarter notes and eighth notes. Let's try it picking all the notes with the thumb. This is demonstrated in the video.

▶ *Video 3*

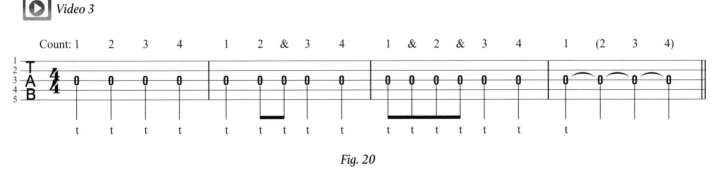

Fig. 20

So, tablature for bluegrass banjo will be written as mostly eighth notes, mixed with occasional quarter notes and rests. We'll talk more about counting as the book progresses.

Fretting

Fretting is the act of pushing the string down to change notes. When tuning, you are bringing the strings to a certain tension, or tightness. The tighter the string, the higher the pitch. Once a given string is in tune (the correct tension), it plays that pitch, or note. If the string is now shortened, but the tension remains the same, it will create a higher pitch. This is what happens when you fret a note. You are pushing the string down at a given a fret, which shortens the vibrating string length and raises the pitch.

The grids used in Figs. 21 and 22 are simple representations of the banjo neck. The numbers across the bottom tell you which string you're looking at; dots placed on the grid indicate finger placement; and letters inside the dots tell you which finger to use.

I = Index; M = Middle; R = Ring; P = Pinky; and, occasionally, T = Thumb

To fret a note, press down with the tip of the finger, *just behind* (to the left of) the fret wire on the neck—not directly over it. Placing a finger on top of the fret wire will deaden the note. The grid in Fig. 21 shows the 3rd string fretted on the 2nd fret, with a tab example below. The black dot with the "M" indicates that you use your middle finger. Fig. 22 shows the 2nd string fretted on the 1st fret with the index finger; again, the tab example is below the grid.

 Video 4

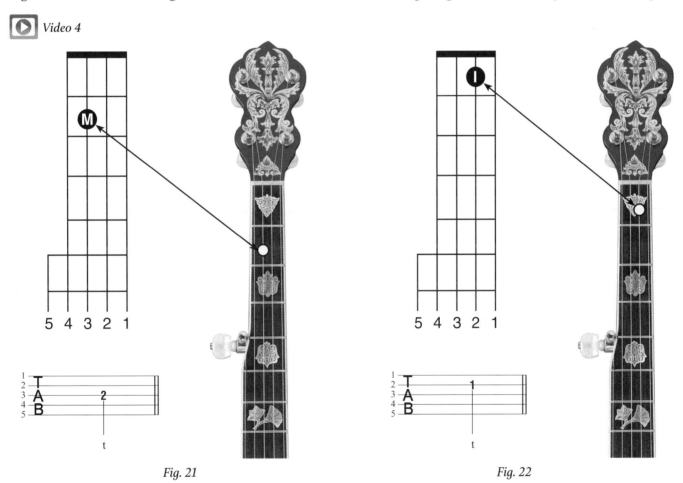

Fig. 21   Fig. 22

On the Staff

As mentioned, each tab line represents a string. The numbers on the lines tell you whether the string is picked open or fretted. Let's look at the examples on the next page, starting with Fig. 23.

 Video 5

- The note appears on the top line, which represents the 1st string.
- The number is zero, meaning that the 1st string is open (not fretted).
- The letter "t" below each note tells you to pick it with your thumb.
- There are numbers above, indicating the beat each note is played on. Remember, these will not normally appear; they are here for instruction.

Now, let's look at Fig. 25.

 Video 6

- Again, we are picking these notes on the 1st string.
- The first two notes (on beats 1 and 2) are on the 2nd fret.
- The second two notes (on beats 3 and 4) are on the 3rd fret.
- The grids below the tab (Figs. 26 and 27) show the positions of the notes on the banjo neck.

Let's check out Fig. 28.

 Video 7

- This time, we're on the 3rd string.
- Each note is played once: open, 2nd fret, 3rd fret, open.
- All notes are picked with the thumb.

While this is not a strict rule, when fretting individual strings, try to match the left-hand finger with the fret. In other words, if it's 1st fret, use the index; 2nd fret—middle; 3rd fret—ring. This is shown in the grids. As soon as you start making chords, this "rule" will no longer apply; but for now, let's follow it.

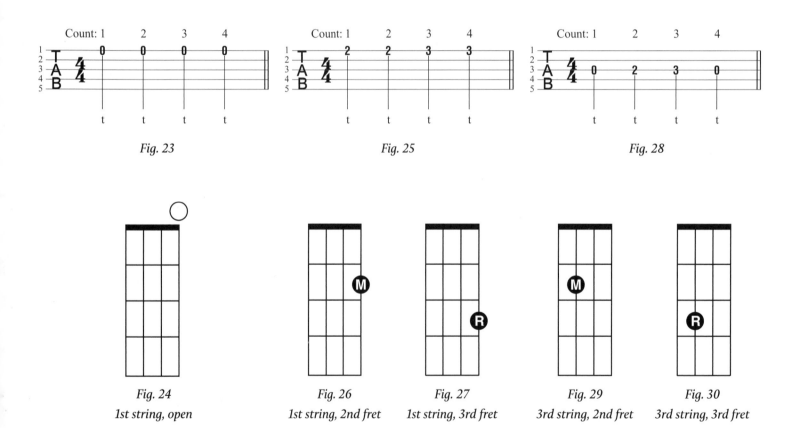

Fig. 23

Fig. 25

Fig. 28

Fig. 24
1st string, open

Fig. 26
1st string, 2nd fret

Fig. 27
1st string, 3rd fret

Fig. 29
3rd string, 2nd fret

Fig. 30
3rd string, 3rd fret

Picking

When picking, the movement of the thumb and fingers is from an open to a closed hand. With the right hand over the strings near the bridge and the planted pinky, the thumb moves downward and the fingers move upward. The videos demonstrating rolls, Videos 8–13, are great examples of the picking hand in action.

Let's Make Some Music

We are going to play a simple tune to get used to how tablature works.

Mama Don't 'Low (Version 1)

We will pick *only* quarter notes, and we will use *only* the thumb. Our main goal here is accuracy. When playing, there are three factors to consider. As mentioned earlier, they are: accuracy, smoothness, and speed—in *that* order. For this exercise, it truly does not matter how fast you play it; what matters is that you play every note correctly. Initially, I suggest that you learn one or two measures at a time. Looking at the first measure (Fig. 31), we see the 2nd string is played three times, and the 3rd string once—all open. Let's play just those four notes, concentrating on accuracy. Now, repeat them several times until they're all about the same duration (same amount of time between them). There's the smoothness. We're not going to worry about speed on this one.

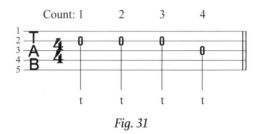

Fig. 31

Now, do the same with the second measure (Fig. 32). When that is as smooth as the first measure, put them together and go for the same smoothness. (The third measure is only one picked note, so it's included in this example.) These nine notes make up the first *phrase*. A phrase is, quite literally, a musical sentence. Once this is smooth, repeat the process with measures 3–6, and so on.

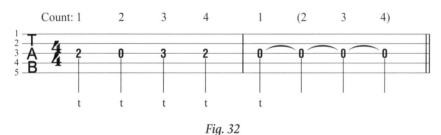

Fig. 32

MAMA DON'T 'LOW (VERSION 1)

Track 1

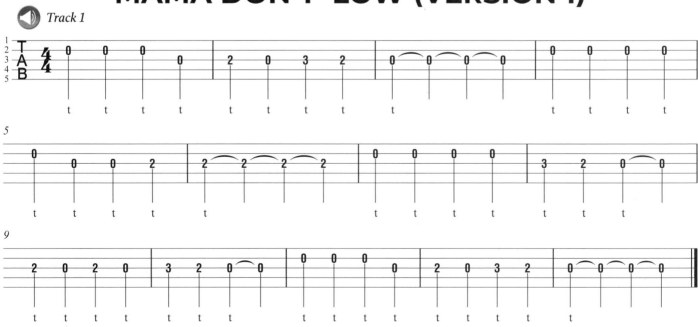

Right-Hand Rolls

Roll is another term for *picking pattern*, a specific combination of notes and strings. There are countless rolls for the right hand, some of which are used in their entirety, some with small variations, some repeated several times, others in portions, and still others in smaller segments tied to other smaller segments. Rolls can be thought of as the framework of almost everything you will play. As you progress, you will add left-hand techniques like chords, slides, hammer-ons, and pull-offs to some of these rolls. There are no solid rules concerning right-hand rolls, but by learning the following patterns, then making small changes as you progress, you'll come to understand the banjo player's approach to rolls.

To begin, we will use each roll as a separate exercise and repeat it—a lot! Once you are familiar with a roll, the idea is to repeat it and to do so without a pause between the end of one and the beginning of the next, in a loop. Earlier, we referred to accuracy, smoothness, and speed. They all apply here. The first thing to focus on when learning a roll is picking the correct string with the correct finger. Smoothness and speed come later. Notice that, initially, all notes are zeros, meaning they are played open. The left hand is not involved yet.

We will be using all three fingers to pick. The letters below the notes tell you which finger to pick each note with. As a reminder:

> t = thumb
> i = index
> m = middle

Roll No. 1: Forward/Backward Roll

The first roll is a *forward/backward roll*. A *forward roll* moves from a lower-pitched note to higher ones; a *backward roll* does the opposite. Fig. 33 is the first half of this roll, the forward part. You will pick the 3rd string with your thumb, 2nd string with index, 1st string with middle, and 5th string with thumb. Play this first half several times until you are able to play it smoothly—not fast, just smooth and even, stressing accuracy! Once it's comfortable, do the same with the second half (Fig. 34). When you can play both at about the same smoothness and speed, put them together (Fig. 35).

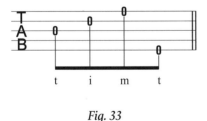

Fig. 33

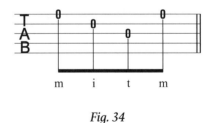

Fig. 34

Finally, when you can play through the entire roll smoothly, start repeating it. Work toward repeating it without any pause between the end of one and the beginning of the next.

 Video 8

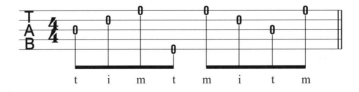

Fig. 35. Forward/Backward Roll

There are several more rolls to learn. I suggest doing the same thing with each and every roll:

- Learn the first half.
- Learn the second half.
- Put them together.
- Repeat the full roll over and over.

You will notice some similarities between certain rolls, too. A few have the same first half, so when you get to those, you'll already be familiar with part of them.

Roll No. 2: Thumb Up/Down Roll

In the *thumb up/down roll* (Fig. 36), the two halves are almost identical, with the exception of one note. In the first half, you pick strings 3, 2, 5, and 1, while in the second half, you pick strings 4, 2, 5, and 1. So, after you get used to the first half, only the thumb changes for the second half; that note is highlighted in the example.

 Video 9

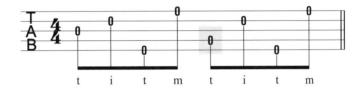

Fig. 36. Thumb Up/Down Roll

Roll No. 3: Forward Roll

Next, we have a forward roll. While the two halves are a bit different, both move in a forward direction. In fact, the first half of this one is identical to the first half of Roll No. 1, the forward/backward roll. Pay particular attention to the first note in the second half (highlighted in the example). It's on the 3rd string, but this time—unlike the first half—it's picked with the index finger, not the thumb.

 Video 10

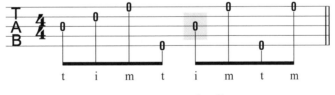

Fig. 37. Forward Roll

Important Note: A general rule is to avoid picking two notes in a row with the same finger, but there are exceptions. If there's a rest between those notes, it works, and there will inevitably be a spot where you have no other choice. Whenever possible, though, you should avoid it. The note just before the highlighted 3rd-string note is on the 5th string, picked with the thumb. It may already be a habit to automatically pick the 3rd string with the thumb, but we must use the index here.

For now, if you notice that you're using the same finger to pick two notes in a row, stop and take a closer look. At this point in time, it is most likely a mistake.

Roll No. 4

Here's another forward roll and a variation, both of which are commonly used. Remember, because they move from lower- to higher-pitched notes, they are forward rolls. The form of the two rolls is almost identical, except that the first version (Fig. 38) starts on and uses the 3rd string, while the second version (Fig. 39) starts on and uses the 2nd string. Again, pay attention because both versions start with the thumb, but when that string is picked again, you use the index finger instead. These notes are highlighted in the examples.

 Video 11

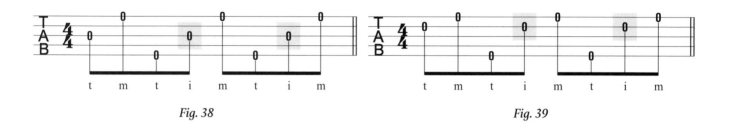

Fig. 38   Fig. 39

TOOLBOX

Vocabulary

This is a good place to introduce some new vocabulary words.

- A *phrase* in a piece of music is much like a sentence in a paragraph. In fact, if the tune has words, one line of the lyrics is often one musical phrase as well.

- A *lick* is a short section, maybe one or two measures, that might serve a purpose like ending a phrase.

- A *riff* is a longer section, perhaps several measures, that repeats. A good example comes from the rock song "Smoke on the Water." That repeating guitar part that's so famous—that's a riff.

Roll No. 5

Here is a variation on the forward/backward roll, and a very important one at that. When we add some left-hand movements to this roll, it becomes what we call a *tag lick*. This particular one is used heavily in bluegrass banjo. When we introduce tag licks (see page 87), we'll come back to this one. Let's give it a go, being careful not to repeat fingers with the picking hand.

 Video 12

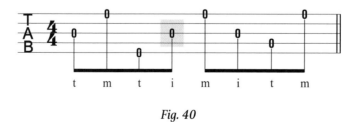

Fig. 40

Roll No. 6

Now we have another important roll. Once left-hand fingerings are added, this roll should sound familiar as the beginning measures of "Foggy Mountain Breakdown." But that's not all—it's widely used as part of a longer lick, often paired with Roll No. 5, when ending a phrase.

Pay attention to the first half. While the 2nd and 1st strings are repeated (2–1–2–1), the picking fingers are not. When you first try this one, it seems easier to just pick with i–m–i–m. But once you start to speed things up, that gets a bit more difficult. By using the thumb (highlighted note in Fig. 41), you will be able to play this much faster and cleaner. So, I suggest repeating the first half a lot to form good muscle memory right away. Trust me, breaking a bad habit in either hand can be a difficult task. Best to get it right the first time.

 Video 13

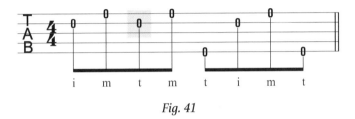

Fig. 41

Roll Exercises

Let's make some exercises out of the rolls we just learned. In the exercise below (Fig. 42), we start with Roll No. 1, playing through it twice. Then, we play Roll No. 2 twice.

We've introduced a couple of new things here, too. Notice the two dots at the beginning of the first measure and the end of the fourth measure. These are *repeat signs*. When you get to the repeat sign in the fourth measure, go back to the opposite-facing repeat sign at the beginning and start over. After repeating, when you come to the sign again, simply continue playing past it (unless there's a note saying to repeat more than once). Sometimes in music notation, a repeat sign will not be included at the start of a song, even though a single repeat appears later. In this case, you would still repeat back to the beginning.

The final measure is a *strum*. Here, you take the indicated picking finger—in this case, the thumb—and brush it across the notated strings in the direction of the arrow.

 Video 14

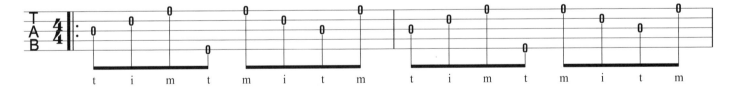

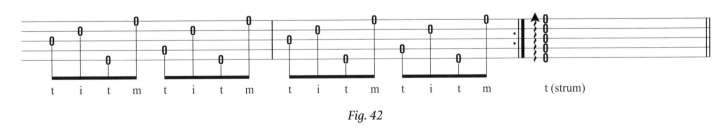

Fig. 42

This is just an example. You can combine any and all rolls and make your own exercises out of them. The goal is to keep a steady pace and to eventually switch from one roll to the next without pausing to think about what's coming next.

Let's do another. This time, we'll play both versions of Roll No. 4. Start with one measure of the original form. Then, do one measure of the variation. Remember, for the variation, we're just moving all the notes from the 3rd string to the 2nd string. Measures 3 and 4 are the same as measures 1 and 2.

 Video 15

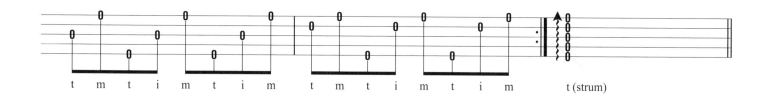

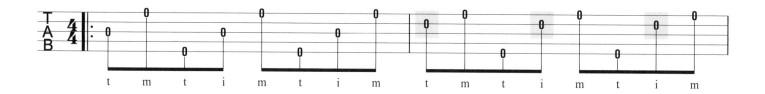

Fig. 43

As explained earlier, the repeat signs tell you to play measures 1 through 4, go to the beginning, play measures 1 through 4 again, and continue. Because this is an exercise, you might consider repeating it over and over many times when practicing.

You can continue this with any combination of the rolls we've learned so far. You can also make variations. Here's one more. This may be a bit more challenging, but later, when we add the left hand, you'll find it's one you'll be using pretty often.

We start with Roll No. 6. In the second measure, we do a variation on that roll, moving all the 2nd-string notes to the 3rd string and picking with the same fingers. In the third measure, we do Roll No. 5, finishing it with a single open 3rd string. As a bit of a departure from the other rolls, notice that each roll here starts with the index finger.

 Video 16

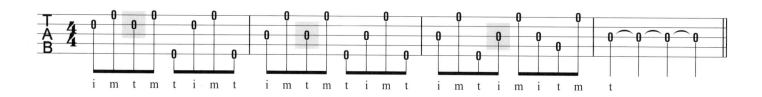

Fig. 44

Chords

Now that we have some right-hand rolls behind us, it's almost time to play some tunes. Before we can, however, we'll need to add a couple of *chords* to our arsenal.

Popular opinion states that a chord is a combination of three or more tones played at the same time. This has been disputed by some, who claim that in many cases, two tones are enough to make a chord and that the brain can infer the third note because of the context in which the two-note chord is being used. Whatever the case, most chords on the banjo involve at least three of the strings.

To demonstrate a chord in this book, we will use the same grid that we introduced in Fig. 21 to demonstrate single fingerings. The only difference is that with chords, you will have several fingers fretting different strings at the same time. While we've discussed this earlier, let's just cover the details again for a refresher. Notice in Fig. 45, on the next page, that the grid is a fairly accurate representation of the banjo neck itself; the vertical lines are the strings and the horizontal lines are the frets. The numbers across the bottom tell you which string you're looking at, the dots on the grid indicate finger placement, and the letters inside the dots tell you which finger to use:

I = Index
M = Middle
R = Ring
P = Pinky
T = Thumb

The thumb is only occasionally used to fret a note, but now and then you may need it for a note on the 5th string. You simply wrap it around the top of the neck to fret the string from the opposite side. Later, in the videos for the Melodic Banjo section, you will see this technique in use.

We will begin with two chords: D7 and C. Earlier, we discussed posture. Let's assume for now that you are sitting while practicing. Remember to sit up straight in an armless chair, like a kitchen or folding chair.

The left hand comes under the neck and should be relaxed with the fingers curved, like you're holding a ball.

Place the tips of the fingers at the designated spots on the fingerboard, making sure that the tips are the only parts of the fingers touching the strings.

When trying a new chord, the first step is to place the fingers. Once they're in the correct position, pick each string slowly, one at a time. They should all sound clean and ring out clearly. If you find you have a dead or muted string, check your left hand to see if one of the fingers is touching another string. If this happens, the finger may be approaching the neck at an angle. Try to arch the fingers by bringing the wrist forward, or a bit more under the neck.

Many tunes can be played with three chords. The 5-string banjo is tuned in a G major chord, so you already have one to work with. In other words, when you strum the open strings, you are playing a G major chord. The first chord we will learn with fretted notes is D7.

D7 Chord

 Video 17

- To play D7, place the tip of the index finger on the 2nd string, just behind the 1st fret (Fig. 45). Notice that the dot indicating the finger is not directly on the fret, there is a little bit of space.

- With that finger in place, place the tip of the middle finger on the 3rd string, just behind the 2nd fret.

- Now, play all five strings, one at a time, and check to see that they're all ringing clearly. If they are, you have a successful chord.

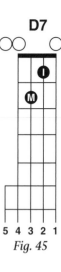

Fig. 45

C Major Chord

Video 18

Major chords can be referred to by only their letter. So, the C major chord is often called "the C chord" or just "C."

- Notice that in a C chord, the index finger is in the same spot as in D7.

- The middle finger is on the 2nd fret of the 4th string.

- The ring finger is on the 2nd fret of the 1st string.

- Again, play all the strings individually to hear if they're all sounding properly.

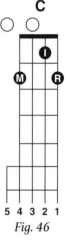

Fig. 46

Congratulations, you now know your first two chords (or three, including the open-string G chord). At first, you will find that you have to think about what you're doing, placing each finger individually. The objective here is to be able to move from one chord to another smoothly, moving all fingers at once, and with as little pause as possible between the chords. The more you change between the chords you know, the sooner the smoothness will come.

For practice, you might strum a D7, then a C, moving between the two repeatedly—and by repeatedly, I mean a lot! When practicing something like this, it is not unrealistic to say you will be doing it thousands of times.

Chord Exercise No. 1

Once you can play the chords, you can work them into exercises with right-hand rolls. At this point, it still doesn't matter how fast you're picking or making the chord changes; we're still going for accuracy.

The following example uses Roll No. 2 (thumb up/down), but I suggest playing through these chords using all the rolls. In fact, make up exercises using different combinations of the chords and rolls.

- At the start, play the roll open (no fingers on the frets) two times. This is a G chord.

- Next, play the roll twice with a C chord.

- Play it twice with D7.

- Play it once more with the open G chord.

- Then, end with a single open 3rd string (as written here) or an open strum.

Video 19

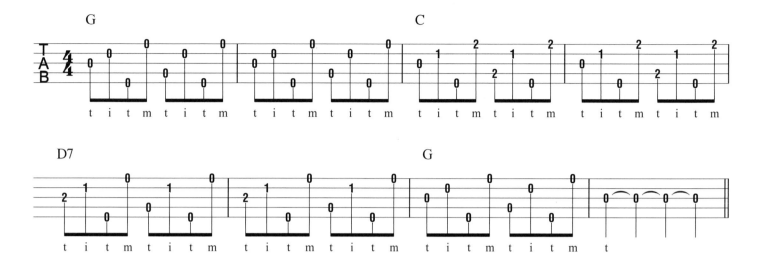

Fig. 47. Roll and Chord Exercise

Feel free to reverse the order of the chords or use different rolls. The idea is to get used to making changes on the fly with a minimum of pauses or stops. Track 2 demonstrates the same exercise as Fig. 47, only using the forward/backward roll.

Track 2

> **TOOLBOX**
>
> **Practice Tips**
> Remember to use the PLAYBACK+ audio player that comes with the audio tracks for this book. You can use it to slow down and/or loop the tracks for listening or playing along—the perfect tool for optimizing your practice sessions!

Counting

We have learned the quarter note, how long it lasts, and why it's called a quarter note. Now, let's talk about *rests*. Imagine a silent note. You still count it; you just don't pick it. This is a rest. A *quarter rest* is one beat of silence, a *half rest* is two beats of silence, and a *whole rest* is four beats of silence. Note: You can stop the previous note from ringing by just touching the string with a right-hand finger or the fingers of your left hand.

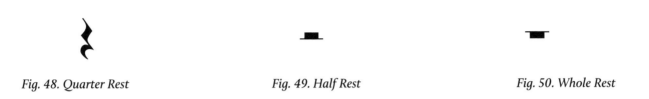

Fig. 48. Quarter Rest   *Fig. 49. Half Rest*   *Fig. 50. Whole Rest*

New Notes

As far as note values, so far you've only learned about quarter notes and eighth notes. For half rests and whole rests, there are also matching notes with these same durations: the *half note* (two beats) and the *whole note* (four beats). Because we usually see banjo notation written on a tablature staff with fret numbers instead of noteheads, often a half note is notated as two tied quarter notes. Similarly, whole notes are sometimes presented as four tied quarter notes

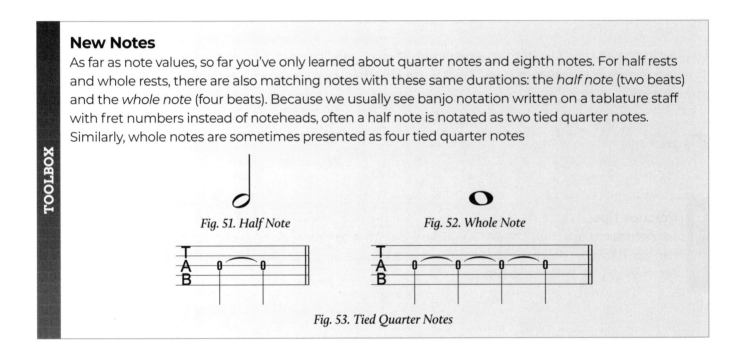

Fig. 51. Half Note   *Fig. 52. Whole Note*

Fig. 53. Tied Quarter Notes

The exercise below consists of three measures, each containing a different combination of notes and rests.

🔊 *Track 3*

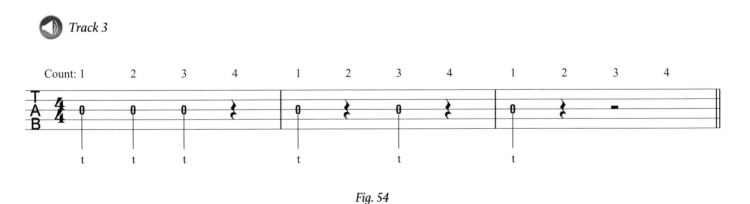

Fig. 54

Mama Don't 'Low (Version 2)

Let's take another look at "Mama Don't 'Low," this time with the proper counting and rests. Remember, the counting numbers for each measure are above the staff. You count every beat in every measure, whether you're playing a note or observing a rest.

MAMA DON'T 'LOW (VERSION 2)

 Track 4

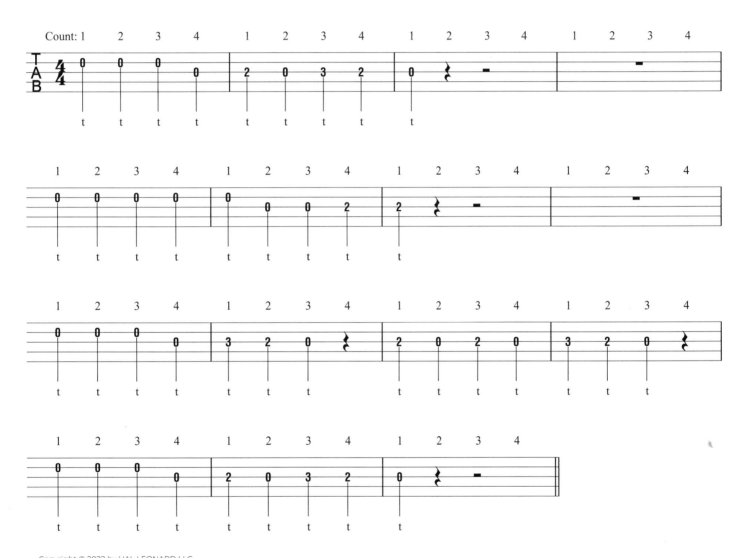

The Real Thing

It's time to learn a few tunes, but first we need to learn a new time signature.

Cut Time

We mentioned earlier that 4/4 is the most common time signature. Because of this, 4/4 is often referred to as *common time* and can be indicated with a large "C."

Fig. 55. Common Time

If we put a line through that "C," it cuts the values in half, making it a 2/2 time signature. Here, we have two beats per measure with the half note getting the beat. We call this *cut time* (Fig. 56), and this is the time signature we will use for most of this book.

Fig. 56. Cut Time

So, in cut time, the quarter notes are treated as eighth notes and the eighth notes are treated as *sixteenth notes*. In common time, there are four sixteenth notes to each beat, and they are counted "1–e–&–a." In cut time, because the eighth notes are treated as sixteenth notes, there are four of them to each beat and they are counted the same way.

Here, we see a full measure in cut time.

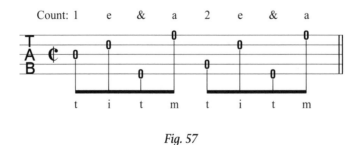

Fig. 57

However, keep in mind that many times it's easier to count these as eighth notes, especially considering the lightning tempo of many bluegrass tunes. Now, let's start working on a tune, for real.

Mama Don't 'Low (Version 3)

We're already familiar with "Mama Don't 'Low," so let's take that a step further and play it with a series of right-hand rolls and chords. Earlier, we talked about learning rolls a little at a time, then piecing them together. It's a good idea to do this with songs, too. The rolls used here should be familiar or slight variations on the rolls we covered, so you might find that you can play two or three measures easily.

Let's look at the first three measures. Measure 1 is already familiar, and so is measure 3. They were two of the original right-hand rolls. Now, look at measure 2. This is a slight variation of measure 3 and has a single fretted note on the second-to-last note of the measure (highlighted).

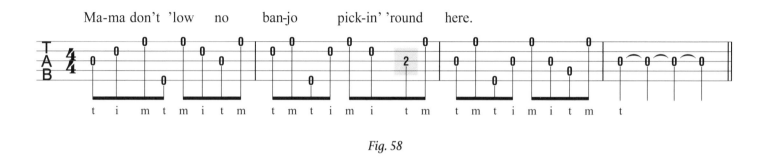

Fig. 58

Stop there. Learn those few measures smoothly. Notice that the first note of measure 3 is the end of the first line of lyrics (see full song). You keep playing for the rest of this measure and all of measure 4, but there are no lyrics there. In earlier exercises, we played one note for every syllable in the lyrics, just like you might do when playing the melody on a piano. In bluegrass banjo, however, we are only approximating the melody and filling in the rest with a lot of notes that fit the chords being played. In this first phrase (Fig. 58), the notes that represent the sung melody are aligned to the lyrics above. Once you're playing a bit smoother, you can try to accent these notes by playing them slightly louder than the others.

So, learn this first phrase (including measure 4), and once that's smooth, learn the next phrase (measures 5–8). Then, put them together. Continue on with this process until you can put all the phrases together. Let's try it.

MAMA DON'T 'LOW (VERSION 3)

 Track 5

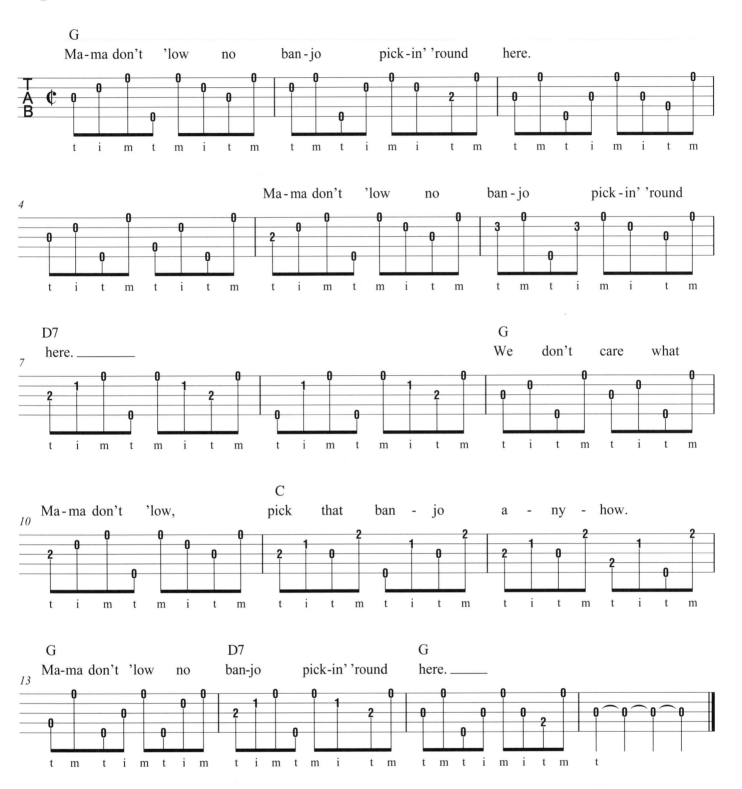

Boil Them Cabbage Down (Version 1)

Here's another standard, "Boil Them Cabbage Down." This mostly consists of familiar right-hand rolls and the basic chords we've learned so far. One thing to keep in mind is that the chords written above the staff are meant for the accompaniment—guitar, mandolin, etc.—not specifically for the banjo. As you are playing through the banjo part and you see a chord symbol, D7 for example, it doesn't mean that you automatically fret the chord with your left hand. Often, you *will* do this, but you have to pay attention to the tab. For instance, there is a D7 chord symbol in measure 4 of this tune, but if you look at the tab, you'll see that the 2nd string isn't picked. You could get away with simply fretting the 3rd string. In fact, the melody is such that you can hold that fret into measure 5, which goes back to G.

In addition, D7 is a mostly major-sounding chord, so the accompanist could play the D7 as written, or a D major chord. This goes for most any 7th chord.

Watch for what happens in measure 8. First, it's all quarter notes; second, we have a couple of *pinches*. A pinch is picking two notes at the same time with the thumb and another finger. They're highlighted in gray in the music. Track 6 will help you with the timing.

BOIL THEM CABBAGE DOWN (VERSION 1)

Track 6

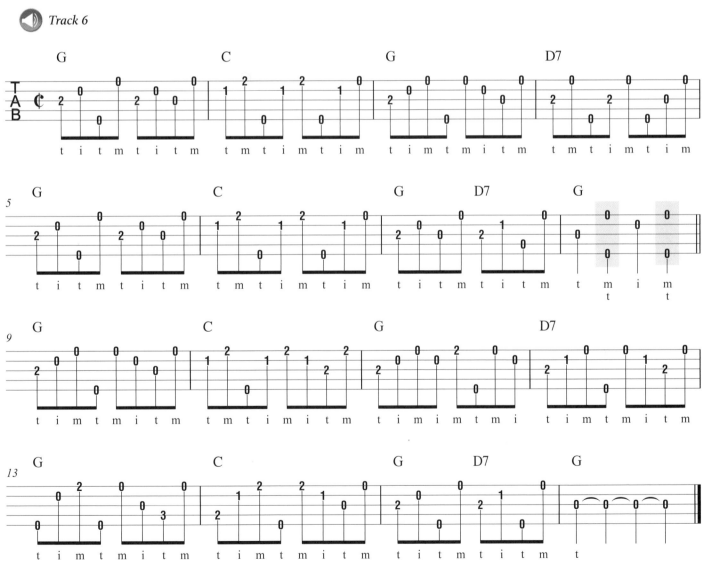

Wildwood Flower

We have a new concept to discuss: the *pickup*. A pickup is a note or group of notes that precede the first full bar of music. Up to now, everything we've played has started on beat 1 of a full measure. This song starts with a half measure, and we think of it as the second half of a measure. If we're counting 1–e–&–a–2–e–&–a, we would start this partial measure on 2–e–&–a, so the 1 happens at the beginning of the first full measure (highlighted in gray). Notice again that measure 3 has a D chord symbol, but all the banjo player needs to do is fret the 3rd string. In measure 8, however, the banjo uses the full chord.

WILDWOOD FLOWER

Track 7

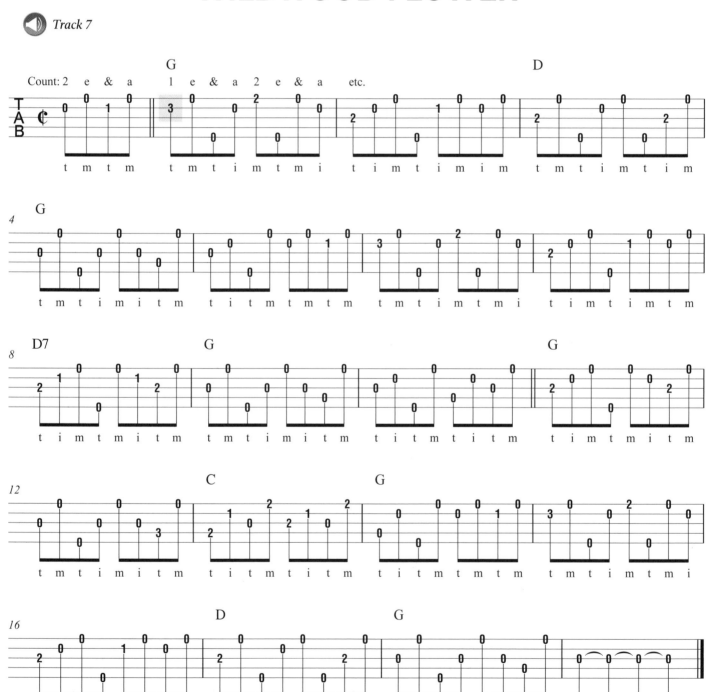

I'll Fly Away (Version 1)

We talked about songs being made up of combinations and variations on the basic right-hand rolls. "I'll Fly Away" is a good example. The first two measures are all variations on the thumb up/down roll. Measure 3 starts with a forward roll and goes into the first part of Roll No. 6. This is followed by a forward/backward roll in measure 4.

Measures 5–8 are all familiar, too. Here, there are slight variations on the strings being picked and the frets or chords being added, but the rolls should all be familiar to you.

As always, practice by learning a few measures, or a line, at a time. As you master the separate parts, add them together until the song is complete.

I'LL FLY AWAY (VERSION 1)
Words and Music by Albert E. Brumley

 Track 8

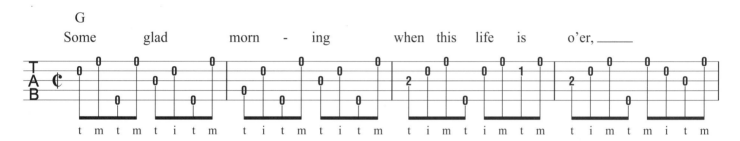

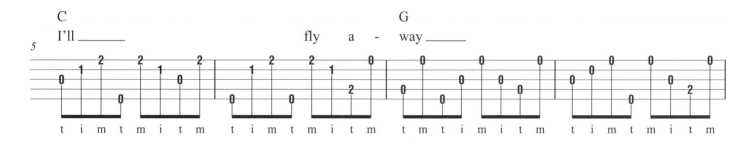

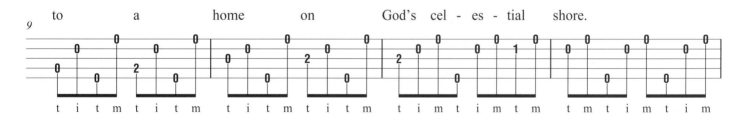

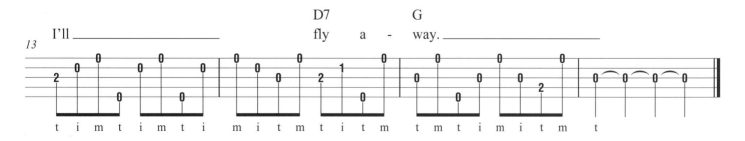

Left-Hand Tricks

Now that we've learned a few songs, we're ready to add some left-hand "tricks," or techniques, to dress up our playing. However, before we do, let's take a look at slurs and a closer look at sixteenth notes.

Slur

The *slur* mark is a curved line connecting two or more notes of different pitches. We use this mark to indicate the left-hand tricks you are about to learn: the slide, the hammer-on, and the pull-off. The slide is shown with a diagonal line between the slid notes and the letters "sl" above to indicate that it is a slide. The hammer-on and pull-off do not use the diagonal line, but do use the letters "h" and "p" above the slur to indicate the move.

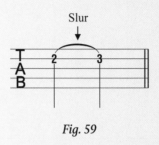

Fig. 59

Sixteenth Note

Earlier, we added a single flag to the quarter note—cutting its value in half—and called it an eighth note. If we add a second flag, its value is cut in half again and we get a sixteenth note (Fig. 60). In cut time, we fit eight of these into every beat. We can use flags on individual notes or beam them together when there are two or more consecutive sixteenth notes.

Fig. 60. Sixteenth Notes

Now, let's get into the techniques themselves.

Slide

 Video 20

The *slide* is indicated with a diagonal line between the fret numbers for two notes. In addition, there is a slur mark above the fret numbers and the letters "sl" above the slur (see Fig. 63). A slide is performed by fretting a note, picking that string, and then moving the finger up to a higher fret on the same string, without releasing pressure with your finger. This creates a continuous unbroken sound that goes from a lower pitch to a higher pitch. On rare occasions, we might find ourselves sliding to a lower note, but because that is so infrequent, we will address only upward slides here.

To begin, we are going to use the first half of Roll No. 1, the forward/backward roll (Fig. 61). Note the counting: 1–e–&–a.

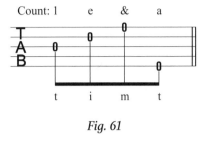

Fig. 61

Now, fret the 3rd string, 2nd fret with the middle finger, and play it again (Fig. 62). The counting remains the same.

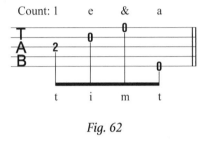

Fig. 62

Finally, we're going to keep the middle finger down but slide it from the 2nd to the 3rd fret after picking it (Fig. 63). The timing of the roll will not change. Do not slow the rhythm of the notes you are picking with the right hand. This slide, which consists of two sixteenth notes, is "snuck in between" the thumb and index notes. The examples below are all demonstrated in Video 20.

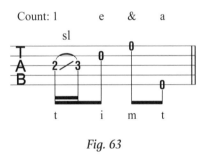

Fig. 63

Now, let's work this into some complete rolls. First, play the entire forward/backward roll (Fig. 64). Then, play the first half of the thumb up/down roll twice (Fig. 65).

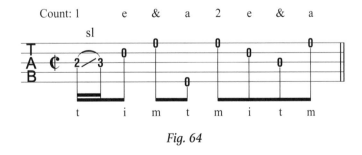

Fig. 64

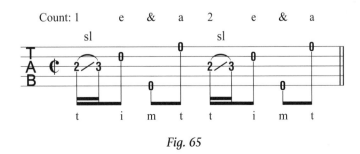

Fig. 65

Hammer-On

A *hammer-on* is named for the motion you make with your finger. It is performed by picking one note—open or fretted—and then sharply bringing down (hammering) a left-hand finger onto the fingerboard to sound a higher note on the same string. We will use hammer-ons with a few of the right-hand rolls we've learned. The hammer-on and slide are timed the same and, on occasion, they might even be interchangeable. Look at the slide example (Fig. 65), and then compare it with the hammer-on version (Fig. 74). As written, they look similar as well, the main difference being an "h" above the slur mark and no diagonal line between the notes.

Let's start with Fig. 66. Begin by simply picking the first note—the open 1st string. Now, bring the middle finger of the left hand down quickly onto the 2nd fret of that same string. When I say quickly, I mean to more or less hit it. You are changing the note not by picking it but by using the finger as a small hammer to quickly change the vibrating string's note without deadening or muting it. If you come down slowly, you will stop the string from vibrating, and the note will not be sounded.

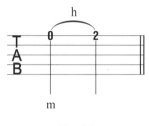

Fig. 66

Let's do another. In Fig. 67, we are doing the very same thing, only on the 4th string.

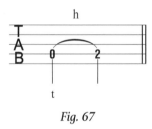

Fig. 67

The example in Fig. 68 is a bit different. This time, we are starting with an already-fretted note and hammering onto another. Fret the 2nd string, 2nd fret with the index finger. Then, pick it and hammer onto the 3rd fret of the same string with your middle finger.

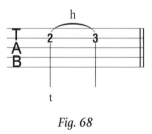

Fig. 68

In practice, the 4th-string hammer-on in Fig. 67 will be played as it is shown in Fig. 69.

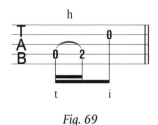

Fig. 69

Likewise, the 2nd-string hammer-on in Fig. 68 will usually be played as it is shown in Fig. 70.

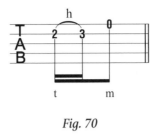

Fig. 70

Taking the previous examples a step further, Figs. 71 and 72 are examples of full measures using the same hammer-ons.

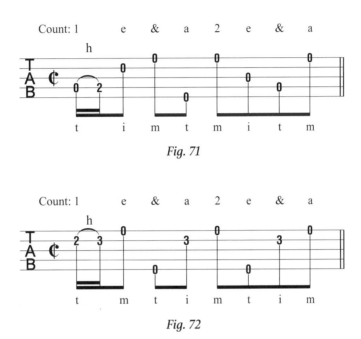

Fig. 71

Fig. 72

Like slides, we will often be playing hammer-ons as sixteenth notes, but not always.

Earlier, we looked at Roll No. 6 (Fig. 41). Now, here it is with a couple of hammer-ons added in. Refresh your memory by playing it a few times open, remembering the right-hand index and thumb placement in the first half, then add the hammer-ons.

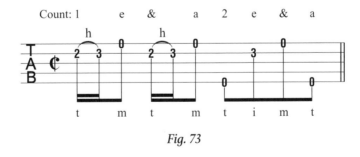

Fig. 73

Also, we mentioned that in some cases, we can interchange a slide and a hammer-on. Here's a good example. First, go back and play the slide example (Fig. 65). Now, do it again, but replace the slides with hammer-ons.

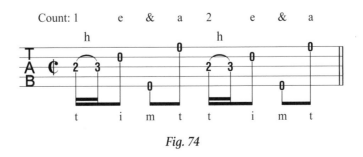

Fig. 74

Pull-Off

 Video 22

The last of our tricks in this section is the *pull-off*. Unlike hammer-ons, a pull-off moves from a higher fret to a lower fret. To do a pull-off, start by picking a fretted note and then "pulling off" (or as described in the video, sometimes "pushing off") of that string with the fretting finger to sound the second note. The pull-off can go to a lower-fretted note on the same string or to the open string. Video 22 covers all the examples below. The pull-off is written in the same style as a slide or hammer-on, but there is a "p" above the slur mark.

The first example (Fig. 75) goes from a fretted note to an open one. Start by fretting the 1st string, 2nd fret with the middle finger. Pick that note and then pull off with your middle finger to sound the second note on the open string.

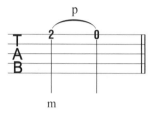

Fig. 75

The second example (Fig. 76) is pretty much the same thing, only on the 4th string.

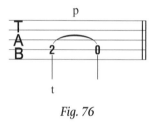

Fig. 76

The third example (Fig. 77) goes from a fretted note to another fretted note. Start by placing both your middle and index fingers on the 3rd and 2nd frets of the 3rd string. Now, pick the 3rd string. Snap the middle finger off, leaving the index finger down on the 2nd fret. In the example, the right hand picks the first note with the index finger. Depending on what's happening before and after, this might be picked with the thumb.

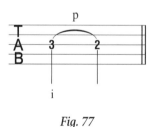

Fig. 77

When learning new techniques or licks, you might consider making up short, repeating exercises. A good one for this 3–2 pull-off would be something like Fig. 79. First, play it open to get the feel for your picking hand (Fig. 78). Notice that the pattern here is similar to the thumb up/down roll. Once this is smooth, add the pull-offs. Remember! You're "sneaking" the pull-off in between the picking of the thumb and middle fingers without interrupting the counting. If you slow your picking hand down to fit the pull-off in, it's wrong. You will add time to that measure, and in a situation when you're playing with others, it will throw everything off.

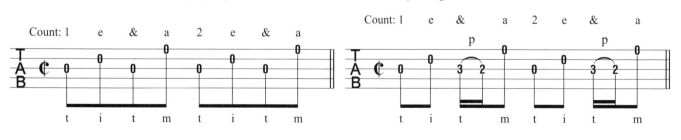

Fig. 78   *Fig. 79*

It's time to add our new left-hand tricks to some of the songs we've been working on; but first, we need to learn a couple of new chords.

D Major Chord

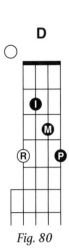

D

You may ask, "What's the difference between the D7 chord that we already know and the D major chord?" Well, the answer could be, a lot, or it could be, very little. For one thing, in traditional banjo music, they can be interchangeable. In terms of music theory, D7 consists of the D chord with one additional note. The two chords are *voiced* a bit differently—which just means how the notes are arranged within the chord—and that alone may be the reason for choosing one over the other. We'll get into some music theory later, but for now, let's just say that a major and a "7" form of a given chord are simply different "colors" of the same chord.

The D chord is fretted with the index, middle, and pinky fingers; and on occasion, the ring finger is included as well (indicated in the diagram with a white dot). Whether we use the ring finger or not in this chord depends on what's happening in the melody. For now, we'll start without the ring and add that later.

Fig. 80

- Place the index finger on the 3rd string, 2nd fret.
- Place the middle finger on the 2nd string, 3rd fret.
- Place the pinky on the 1st string, 4th fret.
- Important: When playing the D chord without the ring finger, which is commonly done, be sure to use the other fingers (I, M, and P) as shown in the grid. Don't substitute! It may seem easier at first, but once you form the habit, it will be difficult to relearn the chord the right way.

As always, play each string individually to be sure they're all ringing out clearly and none are muted or deadened by another finger.

F Major Chord

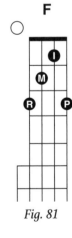

F

While not directly related to D7, the shape of the F chord starts with the same two fingers.

- Start by making a D7 chord: Place the index finger on the 2nd string, 1st fret and the middle finger on the 3rd string, 2nd fret.
- Place the ring finger on the 4th string, 3rd fret.
- Place the pinky on the 1st string, 3rd fret.

Again, play each string individually to be sure that none are muted or deadened by another finger.

Fig. 81

Songs

We'll start with "Mama Don't 'Low" and incorporate some of our new techniques, including slides and hammer-ons, plus the D major chord. Watch the C chord in measure 12. On beat 2, lift the ring finger off the 1st string, leaving the other fingers in place. This creates an interesting sound, adding a little variety. You could just as easily—and correctly—leave that finger where it is.

> **Important Note:** Remember to utilize the PLAYBACK+ audio player to slow down the audio tracks for the following songs. You can play along with the tracks at your desired speed or set loop points to isolate and practice smaller sections of the tune.

MAMA DON'T 'LOW (VERSION 4)

 Track 9

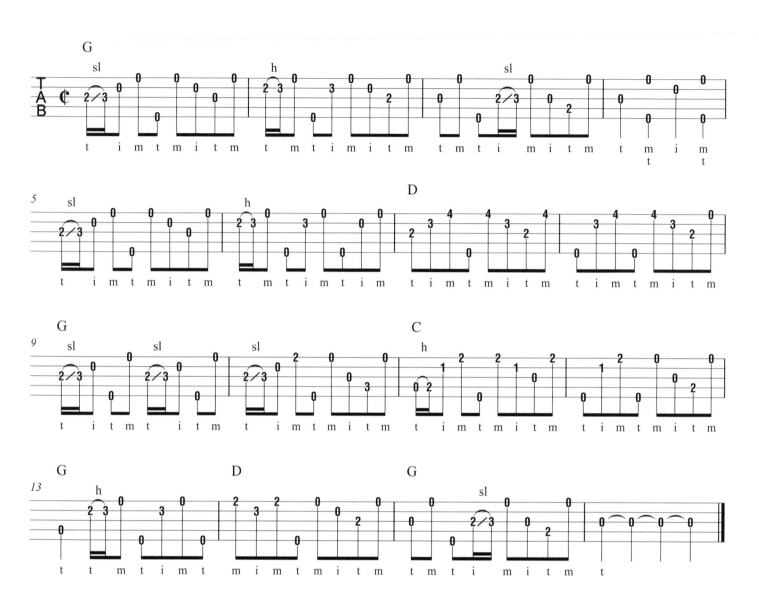

BOIL THEM CABBAGE DOWN (VERSION 2)

 Track 10

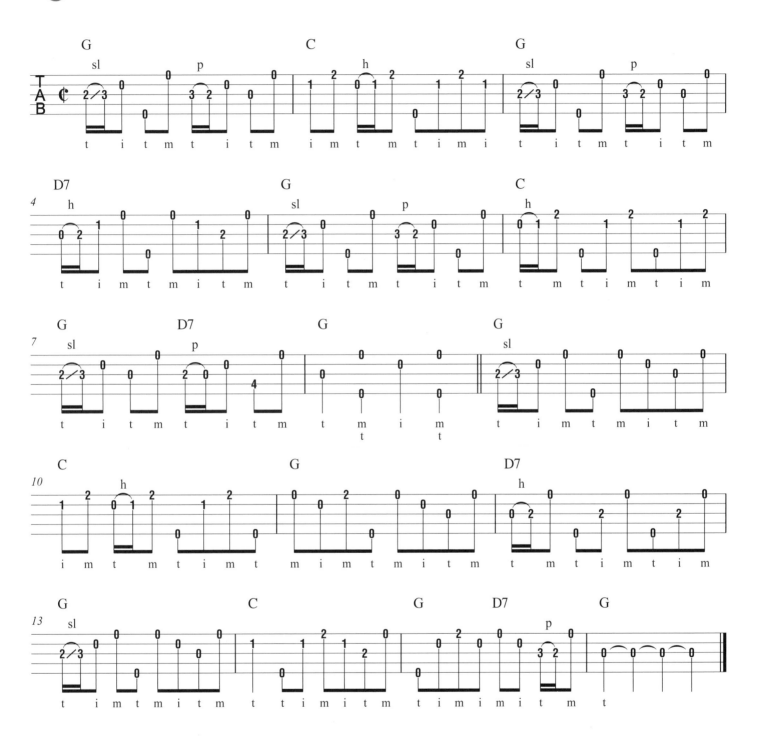

I'LL FLY AWAY (VERSION 2)

Words and Music by Albert E. Brumley

 Track 11

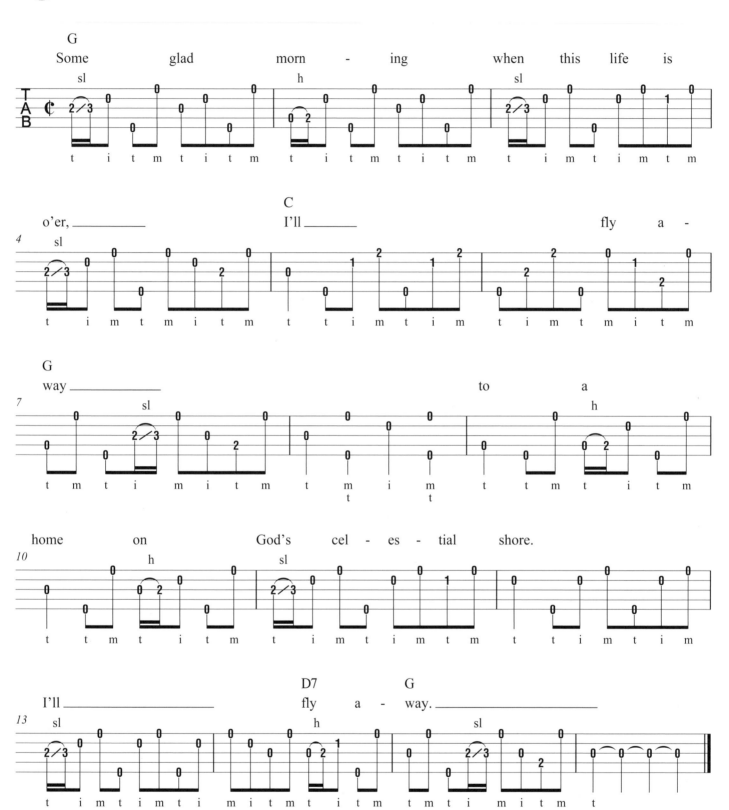

Rhythmic Variations

So far, all the left-hand techniques we've looked at have been played as sixteenth notes, fitting in between the picked eighth notes. This isn't always the case. In the next song, there are several hammer-ons, but notice they are all written as normal eighth notes, just like the picked notes. So, of course, they're also timed exactly like the other eighth notes that are picked. It's an interesting sound that reminds me of a frailing, or clawhammer, banjo style. Listen to the recording and play along.

BURY ME BENEATH THE WILLOW

 Track 12

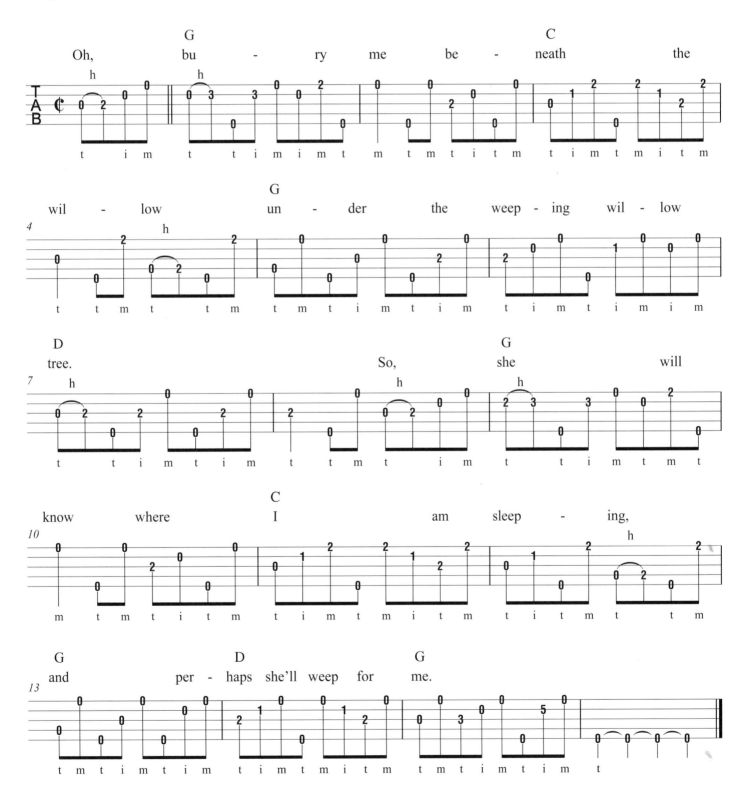

In "Cripple Creek," we have yet another variation on a slide. The very first move in this tune is a quarter note sliding to another quarter note. We start with a pinch—remember, that's two notes played together with the thumb and another finger. Here, the open 5th string is picked with the thumb, and the 1st string, 2nd fret is picked with the middle finger. The next move is a quarter-note slide on the 1st string, from the 2nd to the 5th fret. Then, finish that measure with normal picked quarter notes. This pinch/slide also appears at the end of measure 4. There are additional pinches without the slide throughout the tune.

CRIPPLE CREEK

 Track 13

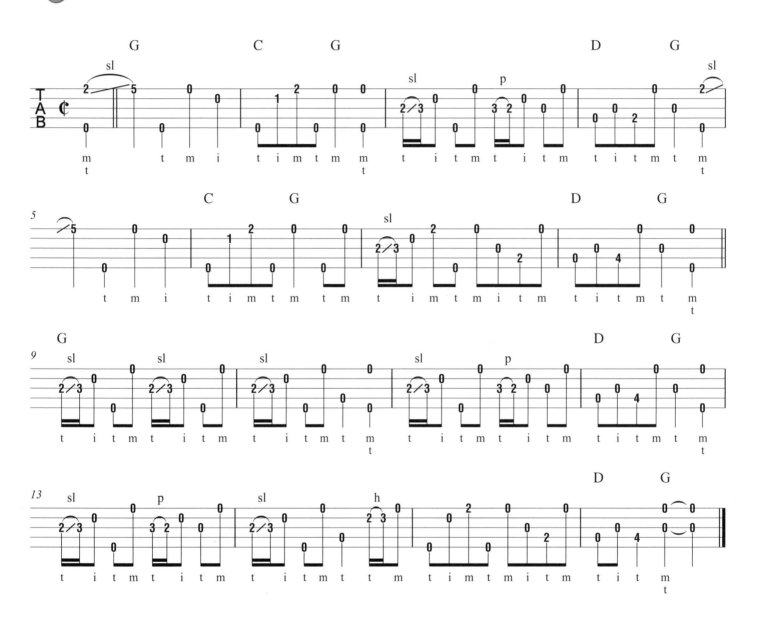

Backup

Another important aspect of banjo playing is what you do when you're not playing the lead part—this is called *backup*, or *accompaniment*. This chapter is divided into three sections: Beginning, Intermediate, and Advanced. I wouldn't advise going through it all at once. Instead, start with the Beginning section and work on that for a while. Then, maybe a month later, work on the Intermediate section, and so on. There's no schedule here. Things that don't make sense now *will* make sense when you're ready for them.

Beginning Backup

In any tune—vocal or instrumental—there are times when the banjo just has to get out of the way so a voice or other instrument can move to the foreground. This is where backup comes in.

At its most basic, you can simply play short, muted chords on the upbeats (the "ands"), keeping the rhythm much like a snare drum would do. Before we start, I suggest you find a favorite bluegrass recording and listen to what the mandolin is doing when it's not playing a solo. It's playing "chops"—short, abrupt chords that serve as a rhythmic backbone.

Also, consider the fact that during a solo break, a mandolin or banjo plays lots of sixteenth notes very quickly; that's a lot of notes in a short amount of time. By going into a backup style, the non-lead instrument is getting out of the soloist's way, making the solo easier to hear. Some banjo players will continue playing rolls behind a mandolin break. They may quiet down a bit, but they're playing every bit as fast as the mandolin, and sometimes, that can become messy. Quite simply, there's too much going on, and it gives the music an overall muddy effect. I'm not saying you can't throw in a tag lick or something here and there, but for the most part, the chops keep the sound clean and might even keep your bandmates happier.

So, with that in mind, there are three important major shapes for backup chords: *D-position*, *F-position*, and the *barre*. These chord forms are all *movable*, because they are made up of only fretted notes—no open strings. Wherever you place these shapes on the fingerboard, you will get a major chord, but it will have a different letter name depending on the location of the chord's *root* note. The root is the note that the chord is built on and from which it gets its name. (We'll get more into the theory of this later.) You have already played D and F chords, and we will move these shapes around to play other major chords.

We'll begin our first example using a D-position G chord. Start by fretting a D major chord. Your index finger is on the 2nd fret of the 3rd string. Holding that position, move it up so that the index finger is on the 7th fret of the 3rd string. It is now a G chord!

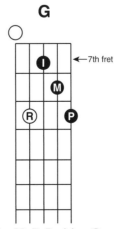

Fig. 82. D-Position G

Let's look at our basic backup rhythm. In cut time, there are two beats in each measure. The bass typically plays on the downbeats (**1**–&–**2**–&–**1**–&–**2**–&), and the backup (chops) are typically played on the "and" of each beat (1–**&**–2–**&**–1–**&**–2–**&**). So, the bass and backup instrument are alternating. (Note: The guitar often does *both* when playing rhythm. A single note is picked on the downbeat, and the rest of the chord is strummed on the upbeat.)

Now, with your D-position G chord in place, switch to an F position, and move up one fret. Your index finger should now be on the 8th fret of the 2nd string, and your pinky should be on the 10th fret of the 1st string. This is now an F-position C major chord (Fig. 83). (Note: Even though we're using an F-position shape, we still just call this a "C chord.") Now, slide that shape up two more frets, and you've got an F-position D chord, with your index finger on the 10th fret of the 2nd string and your pinky on the 12th fret of the 1st string (Fig. 84). To finish this progression, you will go back to a G chord, which might be the original D position we started with, or a barre on the 12th fret. A barre chord is fretted by simply holding one finger across multiple strings on the same fret (Fig. 85).

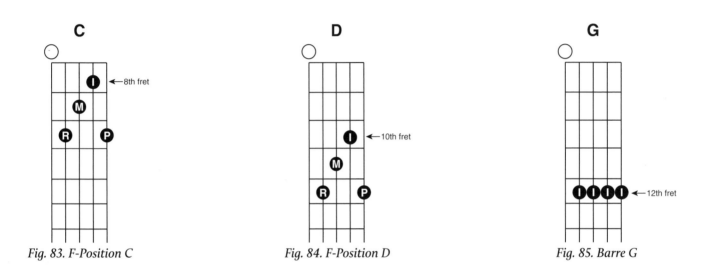

Fig. 83. F-Position C   Fig. 84. F-Position D   Fig. 85. Barre G

Next, we'll look at the basic backup rhythm written out. However, we're going to gradually get away from that and just apply this rhythm to the chord symbols written above the staff in our songs and examples.

In our first example, we're using a D-position G all the way through. We're just getting used to the rhythm here. In the audio, we've added a guitar to help you get the feel for the upbeats and how they sound.

Track 14

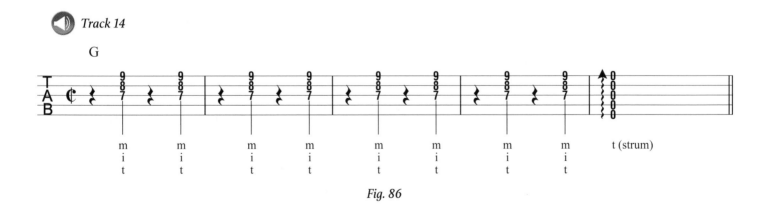

Fig. 86

Now, for the next step, let's change chords. We'll go from G to C to D and back to G. Notice on the C and D chords that even though we're fretting the full chords with our left hand, we can still just play the top three strings.

Track 15

Video 23

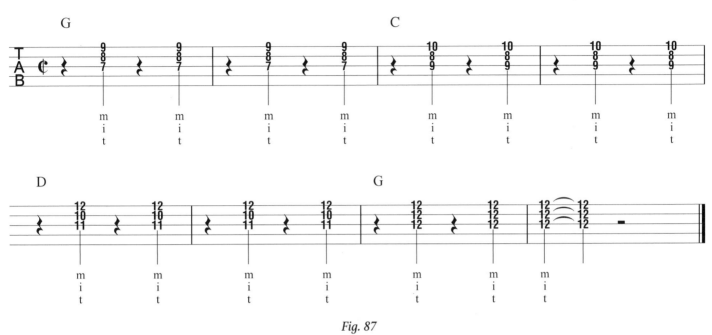

Fig. 87

The next example shows the very same thing, but it's closer to how we'll be thinking of backup from now on. In all tablature, the chords that are being played by the accompanying instrument appear above the staff: for example, the G, C, and D that you see here. This is more of a song *chart*, which shows the essential information but not every detail. Here, the notated rhythm indicates a chord is being played, but you must look above the staff to see *which* chord; in addition, *you* decide what type of accompaniment or picking style to use. Because this is the same as the example above, the audio and video examples apply to both.

Ultimately, after getting the feel, you shouldn't need any written parts. Knowing the chords and some technique should be all you need to play effective backup to any instrument or voice.

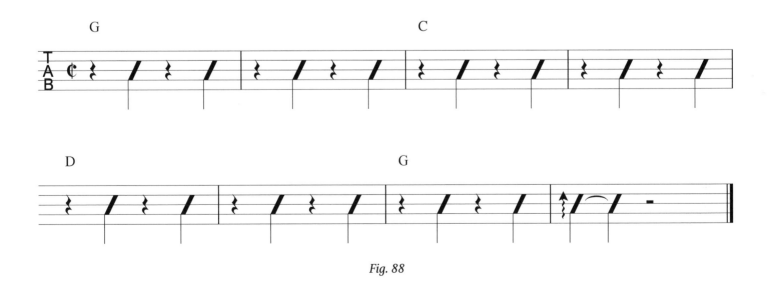

Fig. 88

Backup Theory

In this section, we'll look at some really helpful information for backup playing. It may seem complicated at first, but keep coming back to it; it will eventually make sense!

Key

A *key* is basically the scale (major or minor; more on that below) that a tune is built upon. The key of G is popular because the banjo is tuned so that the open strings play a G chord. So far, everything we've done has been in the key of G.

We will look at scales in more detail in the Melodic Banjo chapter but let's start with some basic information.

Half Step and Whole Step

An *interval* is the distance between two notes. The *half step* and *whole step* are two of the most basic intervals.

A half step is the distance of one fret, either up or down, on the fingerboard.

A whole step is the distance of two frets, either up or down, on the fingerboard.

A *scale* is a series of consecutive notes in a specific pattern of whole steps and half steps.

Major Scale

A *major scale* is the familiar do-re-me-fa-sol-la-ti-do. You can start this on any note, call it "do," and go up from there. The note you start on determines the name of the scale. From the starting note (also known as the *tonic*), you follow this pattern:

whole step–whole step–half step–whole step–whole step–whole step–half step

The notes for a G major scale are G–A–B–C–D–E–F♯–G. Each note is a *scale degree*, and they are numbered 1–2–3–4–5–6–7–8.

do	re	me	fa	sol	la	ti	do
G = 1	A = 2	B = 3	C = 4	D = 5	E = 6	F♯ = 7	G = 8

The Primary Chords

So, if we play a chord built on a given scale degree, we can refer to that chord by its number. We use Arabic numerals (1, 2, 3, etc.) for scale tones; we use Roman numerals (I, II, III, etc.) for the chords built on those scale tones in any given key.

Notice that the first note of the G major scale is G, the fourth note is C, and the fifth note is D. So, in the key of G, the I chord (one chord) is G, the IV chord (four chord) is C, and the V chord (five chord) is D. These three chords, in any key, are so common they are known as the *primary chords*.

Using the Capo

A *capo* is a clamp placed across the fingerboard to raise the pitches of the strings. Let's imagine we're playing with a few other instruments, and the tune happens to be in a key other than G, like A. The bass, mandolin, and fiddle do not use a capo. However, the banjo and guitar probably *will* use a capo in the new key. So you put the capo over the 2nd fret—bringing the overall pitch up to A—but you still play as though the tune is in G. The capo acts as a new nut, so when you place it at the 2nd fret, the notes on the open strings are raised a whole step (two frets); now, the open strings form an A chord. However, you're still *thinking* as though you're in G.

When the mandolin takes a solo, it will be playing over the A (I), D (IV), and E (V) chords. If the mandolin player calls out an A chord, you'll have to transpose that quickly, because you're playing as though you are in G. But if he says "I," you'll have no problem getting to the right chord, which will be A (even though you're thinking G).

The table below gives you the I, IV, and V chords in several commonly used keys. Of course, there are other chords built on the other scale degrees (some are minor), but for now, we'll just concern ourselves with these. (Note: When the Roman numerals are uppercase, they are major chords. Lowercase Romans signify minor chords.)

Number	Key of G	Key of A	Key of C	Key of D	Key of E
I	G	A	C	D	E
IV	C	D	F	G	A
V	D	E	G	A	B

In time, you will start to recognize the chord number by how it sounds in relation to the others. I use song examples to associate the chord numbers with how they sound. For instance, the opening chords in "Dueling Banjos" are I–I–I–IV–I. Departing from bluegrass for a moment, the riff in "Louie Louie" is I–I–I, IV–IV, V–V–V, IV–IV.

QUIZ

In the key of G, what are the chords we'd play for the song examples just mentioned?
What are they in the key of A?

(The answers are at the bottom of this page.)

From this point on, some musical examples will use the Roman numerals for the chords. This is to get you used to being able to play backup in any key with the use of the capo.

Intermediate Backup

There is more to backup playing than just the upbeats we saw in Fig. 87. We can do lots of fancy moves like slides, fill-in licks, and more. We mentioned "getting out of the way" of the lead player—and this is important—but it depends on the situation, too. A mandolin plays just as many notes per measure as a banjo, so stopping your rolls and doing mostly chops is a good idea.

On the other hand, a fiddle tends to play longer, drawn-out notes, which don't clash as much with rolls being played on the banjo; in addition, when the fiddle is soloing, the mandolin is probably already playing chops, so that rhythm part is already there and doesn't have to be doubled by the banjo. Let's take a look at another chord progression (Fig. 89 on the next page) but dress it up a little.

The first thing to notice is the last chord in measure 2. We start the exercise with a D-position G chord for the first few beats. On the last chord in measure 2, we keep the pinky on the 9th fret but go to an F position, sliding it up one fret into measure 3, making it a IV chord.

We maintain the steady chop rhythm until measures 7 and 8, where we throw in a lick on the V chord. Here, the left-hand index finger barres the first two strings at the 12th fret, and the middle finger frets the 14th fret of the 3rd string. The right hand plays a simple backward roll.

Measures 9–12 are exactly the same as measures 1–4. Then, we finish with a fancy tag lick starting at measure 13. Be sure to check out the audio and video to hear how this should sound.

"Louie Louie" in A: A-A-A, D-D, E-E-E, D-D
"Louie Louie" in G: G-G-G, C-C, D-D-D, C-C
"Dueling Banjos" in A: A-A-A-D-A
"Dueling Banjos" in G: G-G-G-C-G

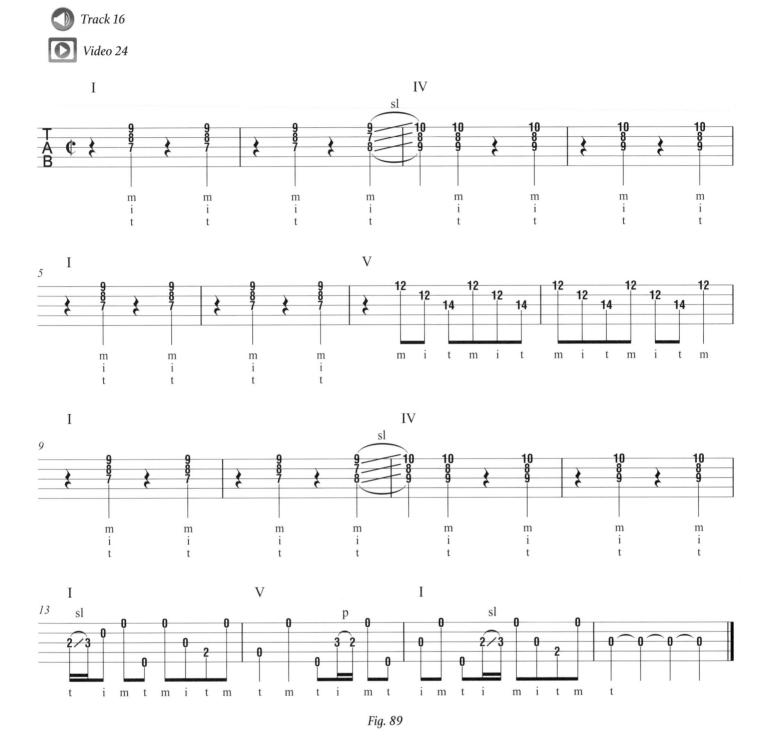

Track 16

Video 24

Fig. 89

Minor Chords

Let's not forget the minor chords. Like major, there are three movable positions: Am, Dm, and Em. This means that the shapes of these basic chords will be a minor chord wherever you place them on the neck, and the frets they are on will determine which chord they are. In backup playing, I typically use only the first three strings. Here are the minor chord positions:

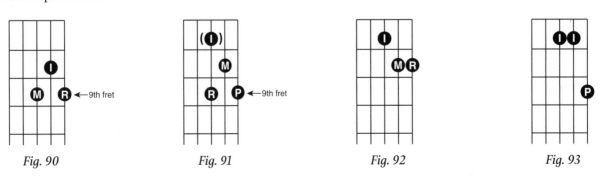

Fig. 90   *Fig. 91*   *Fig. 92*   *Fig. 93*

Figures 90 and 91 show two versions of the Am position. It helps to have a few fingering options for common chord changes, such as moving to an Am-position Em chord from a G chord. For instance, if you're in a D-position G chord, you can just place the ring finger of the chording hand on the 9th fret of the 3rd string (Fig. 91), and voilà, it's an Em. Nothing else has to change. The ring finger is above the index on string 3 so that is the note that sounds, and the index can just be left where it is.

Notice that no frets are specified in Figs. 92 and 93. The chord you produce depends on the frets you're playing. For example, any D-position major chord becomes a minor version of the same chord by simply lowering the 1st-string note by one fret (Fig. 92).

Advanced Backup

Important Note: Let the Intermediate Backup information solidify before starting this section. I suggest working on the intermediate material for days, weeks, or even months before trying the advanced material.

The fancier the backup parts get, the more we have to consider whether or not we will be in another instrument's way. I find that when someone is singing a verse, the banjo can be a little "busier" in the backup department—keep it quieter than during a solo, but you can still show off a bit, particularly at the ends of phrases. When the singer takes a breath, you can throw in a nice lick. In addition, on each verse of a song, the instruments might take turns doing some fancy fill-ins. For instance, if the banjo kicks off the song, the mandolin might do a fill during the first verse, the fiddle might play a fill on the second verse, and the banjo might finish up with backup on the third verse. One more chorus and the song ends. This is something you can learn by listening to lots of recordings!

Think of What You've Done

Let's check out a verse and chorus of "Think of What You've Done" with some banjo backup. On the next pages, notice that the banjo is all over the neck here—both high and low. Don't let that alarm you. In spite of all the high fret numbers, it's mainly working out of D- and F-position chords.

There are a few things to watch out for. In measures 5 and 6, you're working out of an F-position D chord, but the first note of measure 6 is on the 12th fret, when it's normally on the 11th. Simply fret that note with the ring finger.

The next spot to work on is measures 15 and 16. In measure 15, you're playing a D-position G chord. The first note of measure 16 is on the 10th fret, which you would fret with your ring finger; this is a bit of a stretch, so you *could* just leave it as it was in the previous measure, but the last three notes of measure 16 switch to an F position in anticipation of the next measure (F-position C). At first, this may be a bit tricky, and you can simply stay in the D position until measure 17. However, if you want to try it as written, on the fifth note of that measure (indicated with the *), quickly switch to an F position with your pinky remaining at the 9th fret. Then, in measure 17, slide the whole chord up a fret into the C chord. Slow the audio down so you can really hear what's going on.

Notice measure 19. There are three notes (2nd string, 10th fret) that are followed by upward arrows. The arrows indicate a technique called a *choke* (also known as a *bend*). To do a choke, simply pick the note, then, keeping your finger firmly on the fretted string, push that string upward. You are stretching the string and making the note go a bit sharp or high. Take a look at Video 25, as this technique is easier shown than explained in writing. Chokes are also covered in the Tricks section near the end of the book.

 Video 25

Something else to watch out for is in measure 23. You're playing a D-position G here, but on the last three notes, you slide that position down one fret; then in measure 24, you slide down one more. You're actually going from a G to an F chord, anticipating the C in measure 25. If this is too much at first, just continue the roll with the D-position G until you get to the C.

THINK OF WHAT YOU'VE DONE

Words and Music by Carter Stanley

 Track 17

 Video 26

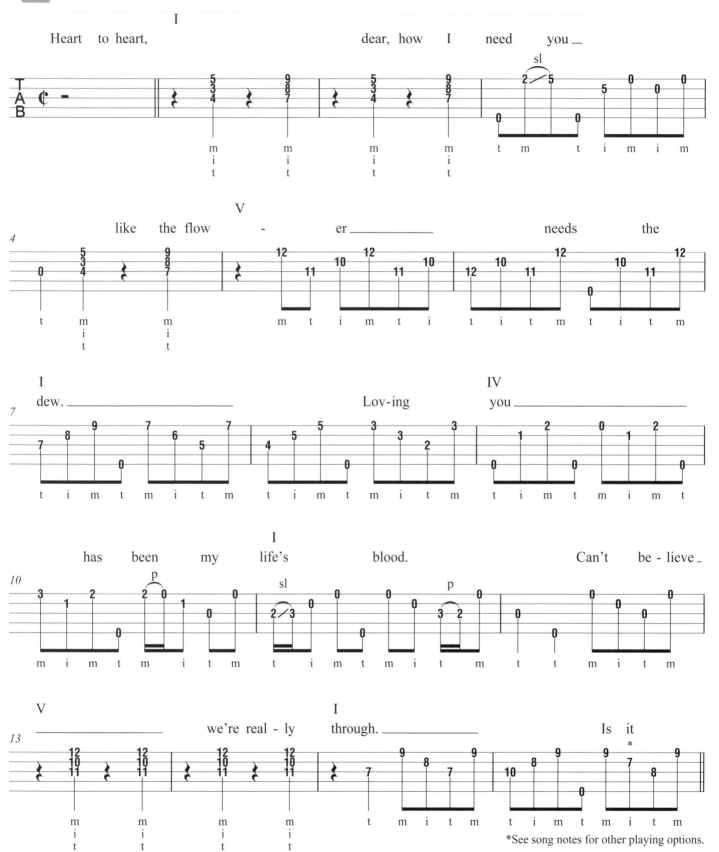

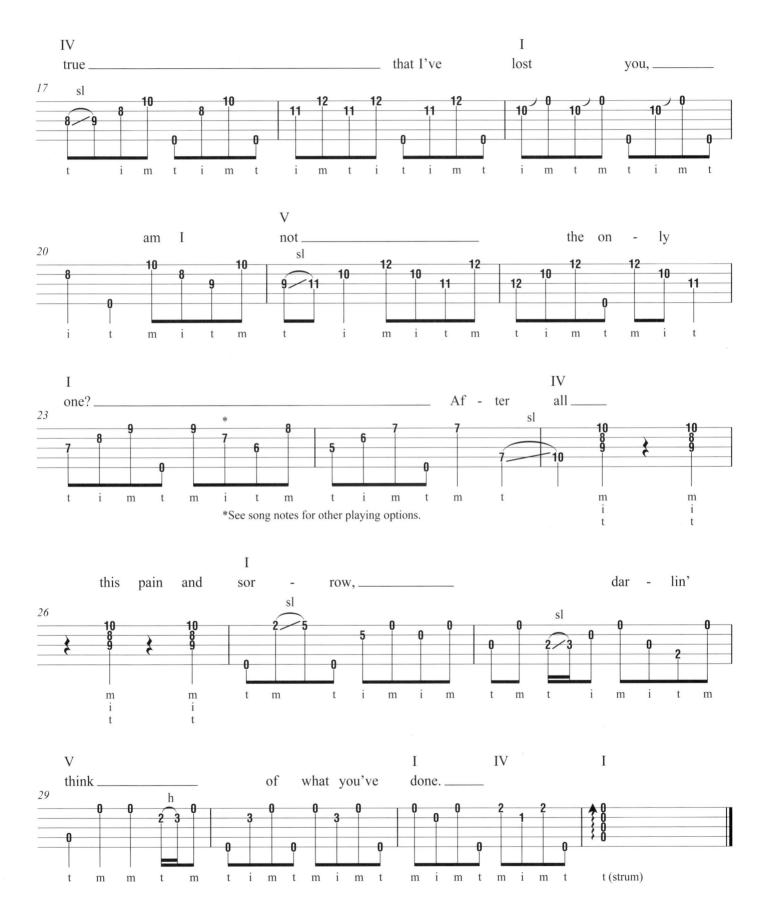

Some More Music Theory

We have discussed certain aspects of music theory already; now, it's time to go a bit deeper. Music theory can be intimidating for some, but it's actually quite interesting and useful. Traditionally, theory has been taught as a set of standards that are either right or wrong, just like math or science. This isn't completely true. Actually, as music developed over the centuries, people paid attention to what was considered acceptable and decided that was "correct." Then, they figured out the mechanics of the accepted ideas and taught it to the rest of us, just like any other language. So, even though "rules" can be flexible sometimes, music theory provides a set of standards and concepts that can give us a greater understanding of what's happening behind the sounds we hear.

Major Scale Revisited

Remember, a major scale contains a series of whole steps and half steps. There are eight notes, or scale degrees, in the major scale, and they're numbered 1 through 8. The 8 is the same note as the 1, just one *octave* higher. (An octave is the distance of 12 half steps from one note to another note with the same name: for instance, from G to the next higher G.)

Fig. 94 shows a G major scale played entirely on the 3rd string. The do-re-me syllables (also known as *solfege*) are above, and the scale degrees are above that. As a reminder, the first two scale degrees go from the open string (or 0) to the 2nd fret. This is a whole step. The 2nd to 3rd degrees are also a whole step. The interval between the 3rd and 4th scale degrees (4th to 5th fret) are only a half step apart (marked with a bracket). And this continues on.

There are better ways of playing a major scale than what we see here, but this is a good way to clearly show the intervals used to build a major chord.

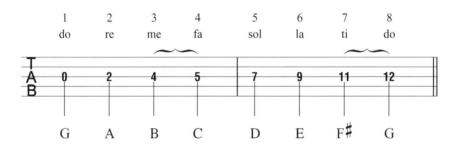

Fig. 94. G Major Scale

Chord Theory

A major chord is built using the 1st, 3rd, and 5th scale degrees of a major scale. So, a G major chord would consist of the notes G, B, and D. If we play the 3rd, 2nd, and 1st strings open, together, that is a G major chord. Remember, the banjo is tuned to a G major chord. The 4th string is another D and the 5th string is another G.

G Major Scale   **G Major Chord (I)**

G A B C D E F# G → G B D
1 2 3 4 5 6 7 8   1 3 5

Fig. 95

The notes of a chord can be stacked in any order, and any note of the chord can be doubled or even tripled and it is still the same chord. These different arrangements of chord tones are called *chord voicings*. For example, instead of playing the 3rd, 2nd, and 1st strings open, try the open 2nd, 1st, and 5th strings. The notes are in a different order and there is a higher G note (5th string open), but all the required notes for that chord are present, so it is still a G chord.

The C major chord consists of the notes C, E, and G.

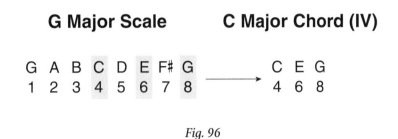

Fig. 96

Diatonic Harmony Revisited

As we saw in the Beginning Backup section, many tunes consist of only three chords (the primary chords). For example, in the key of G, you can do a lot with G major, C major, and D major chords. However, chords can be built on every step of the major scale. What's more, if you adhere to the "rules," some of these chords are major and others are minor and diminished. This approach to understanding chords is known as *diatonic harmony,* which is just the theory of chords that belong to a key.

So, we know that the primary chords of a key are the chords built on the 1st, 4th, and 5th degrees of the major scale. And when we refer to these chords, we use Roman numerals: I, IV, V. In the key of G, the primary chords are G (I), C (IV), and D (V). Remember, major chords use uppercase Romans and minor chords use lowercase. If we were to build a chord on every note of the major scale, we would get the following series of chords: I, ii, iii, IV, V, vi, vii°, I. (The degree symbol after vii indicates a diminished chord.)

So, if we were to build a chord on each note of the G major scale, we would get the following chords:

I	ii	iii	IV	V	vi	vii°	I
G	Am	Bm	C	D	Em	F#°	G

This knowledge will come in very handy in the next chapter on using a capo.

Major and Minor Chords

We've mentioned major and minor chords quite a lot. While there are mathematical formulas for how these chords work, I'd prefer to describe how they sound and feel. We'll play a few examples and hopefully you will understand the difference.

In a nutshell, major chords sound brighter, happier, or more cheerful; minor chords, on the other hand, sound more serious, ominous, or sad.

Some tunes in major keys might occasionally use a minor chord, like a vi, but it's part of a larger picture, and a few beats of a minor chord have little effect on the overall mood of a song.

If you have a song in a minor key, like A minor, that's another story. Bluegrass music includes lots of sad or serious tunes about lost love, death of loved ones, and even murder ballads. Look up "Pretty Polly" and you'll see what I mean.

I think the best way to understand the difference is to play the major and minor versions of a given chord and listen to that difference.

In addition, "Down the Road" (the next song we'll play) and "There Is a Time" (in the Playing in Different Keys chapter) are good examples. "Down the Road" is in a major key and is a fairly upbeat tune that uses an occasional minor chord (vi, or E minor). In this context, it does not darken the feel. "There Is a Time," on the other hand, is in the key of E minor, and while not a sad song, it is definitely more serious—both in the feel of the music and the words.

Roman Numerals

As a reminder and a bit of new information:

- When referring to major chords, we use the letter by itself—like G.
  - When using Roman numerals, major chords are uppercase—like I, IV, and V.
- Minor chords consist of the letter and a lowercase "m"—like Am.
  - When using Roman numerals, minor chords are lowercase—like ii, iii, and vi.

Some New Chords

The vi chord is used a lot in major keys. In G, this is E minor, or Em. Let's try both the major and minor versions of E.

E major is formed much like a C chord, except that the index finger is on the 3rd string instead of the 2nd (Fig. 97).

E minor is similar to E major, except that the index finger is not used at all (Fig. 98).

A minor is again similar to C, except that the middle finger is on the 3rd string (Fig. 99).

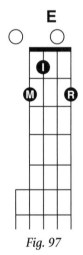
Fig. 97

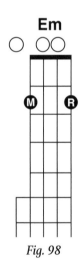
Fig. 98

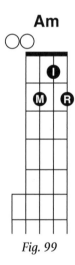
Fig. 99

Down the Road

There's nothing too surprising in this song aside from the new Em (vi) chord. One other thing to watch for is that the time signature changes to 3/2 for measures 7 and 16. So for those two measures, you are playing three beats instead of two. This can feel a bit uneven, so be sure to listen to the audio track.

DOWN THE ROAD

Track 18

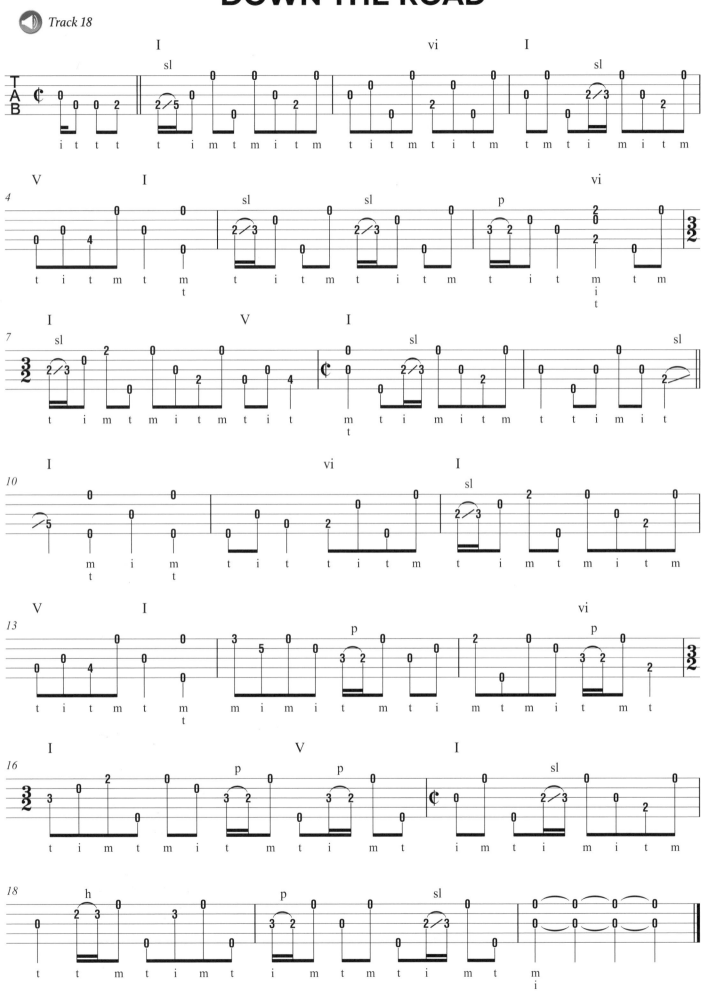

Using the Capo

Remember, a capo is a device used primarily by banjo and guitar players. It allows them to play in different keys while continuing to play in a style that relies heavily on open strings. It is a simple clamp that goes across the neck, holding the strings down at whatever fret the user needs, essentially re-tuning the instrument to a higher key. In other words, it allows you to play in different keys without changing the fingering.

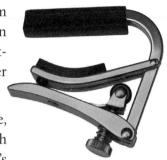

Why different keys? Keys like A and B are popular with vocalists, and believe me, playing bluegrass on a banjo in the key of B without a capo would be, well, pretty much impossible. So don't be hurt if your bandmates call it a "cheater." It's not. If anything, it's more of an "equalizer."

Fig. 100. Capo

A capo is simple to use. Put it on the correct fret. The capo now becomes the nut, so you just play from there in a position and with a fingering you already know. If you want to play in A, put the capo on the 2nd fret, and play like you'd play in G. Everything will be pretty much the same, but the frets are just slightly narrower and you're playing up a whole step in a new key.

OK, there's one important point. On the banjo, you have a 5th string, which starts on the 5th fret. If you look, you'll see that the 5th string has its own nut (Fig. 101). This means that the 5th string will need to be capoed separately, starting from its own nut.

There are several choices for a 5th-string capo—everything from commercially-made attachments with a small extension that can slide up or down to the desired fret and then be clamped down, to tiny model railroad spikes, which are little L-shaped nails that hide right behind certain frets, allowing you to clip the string underneath. I've even seen one made from the cap of a Bic pen. Whatever you use, I suggest getting a professional banjo repair person to install it (well, maybe not the pen cap!). I have seen the results of attempting this job at home, or hiring a repair person who's never done it before; nothing is more painful than a nasty scratch or an extra hole in your beautiful banjo neck.

If you're going to play with others, the capo is necessary; but again, please be sure to have it installed properly. Placement and tightness of the capo are important. If it's too tight, it can pull the strings out of tune; if it's too loose, the strings might buzz. Just like when you're fretting with your fingers, it should be placed just behind the fret, not actually on or over the fret. It's a good idea to check your tuning again after you've placed the capo.

There are many different capos out there, both for the main strings and for the 5th string. I suggest browsing the web for "banjo capo" and "5th-string banjo capo."

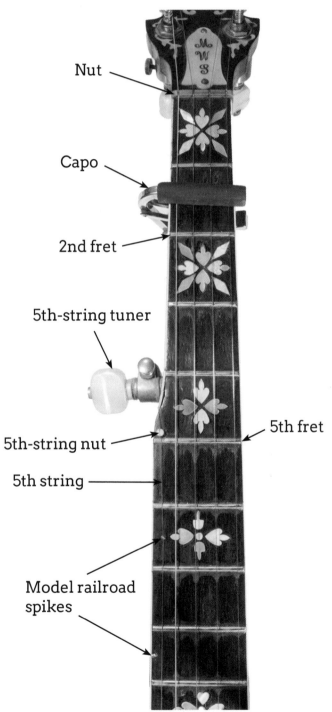

Nut

Capo

2nd fret

5th-string tuner

5th fret

5th-string nut

5th string

Model railroad spikes

Fig. 101. Banjo with Capo on 2nd Fret

Melodic Banjo

Up to now, we've been playing in a pretty traditional style where we approximate the melody while following the chord progression of the tune.

A nice contrast to this style is something we call *melodic playing*. Melodic style is a more stepwise or scale-like style that allows us to more closely play a melody or to replicate other instrumental styles like the fiddle or mandolin.

Playing the Major Scale

Earlier, we talked about major scales, you know, the do-re-me stuff. Fig. 94 showed a G major scale on a single string. It served its purpose there, allowing you to hear it and see how the notes related to one another, but it's not a practical way to play that scale. We'll break it up into two parts, starting with the first five notes: do-re-me-fa-sol. Let's start with the right hand and play an open pattern (Fig. 102). This starts with the index finger picking the 3rd string. Repeat it several times.

Next (Fig. 103), we use the same picking pattern but fret two of the notes. Use the ring finger to fret the 7th fret of the 4th string, then jump to the index finger to fret the 5th fret of the 3rd string.

Now let's take it a step further and go from do to sol and then back down to do (Fig. 104). As always, repeat this several times until you can play it smoothly.

 Video 27

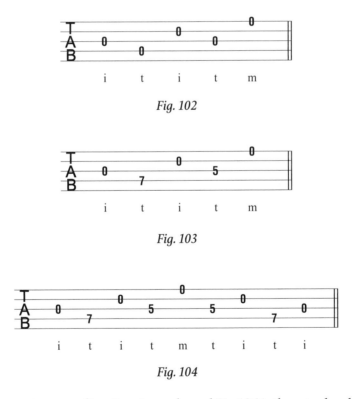

Fig. 102

Fig. 103

Fig. 104

Fig. 105 is the open roll for the entire ascending G major scale, and Fig. 106 is the actual scale with the proper fingerings.

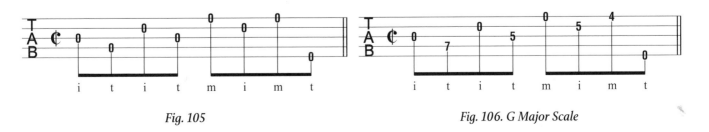

Fig. 105

Fig. 106. G Major Scale

And finally, we have the entire G major scale, ascending and descending (Fig. 107). We even threw in a high A note just to keep it interesting (highlighted). Use the pinky to fret that one.

▶ *Video 28*

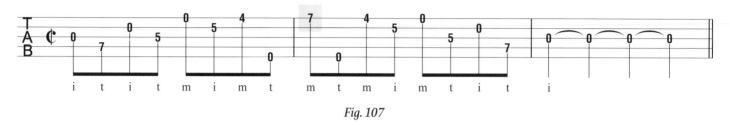

Fig. 107

You may notice in the video that I use different fingers to fret the 4th and 5th strings on the way up than I do on the way down. That's a habit I've formed. You can use whatever is comfortable for you.

Exercises

As you work through the melodic style, you'll see that the left-hand fingering isn't terribly difficult, but the picking can be challenging. Here are some exercises to help with right-hand accuracy. The index and middle fingers will jump to some strings that might be unusual compared to what we've been doing so far.

I use Melodic Warmup Exercise No. 1 (Fig. 108) every time I play. I repeat it 15 to 20 times—each time slightly faster than the last.

▶ *Video 29*

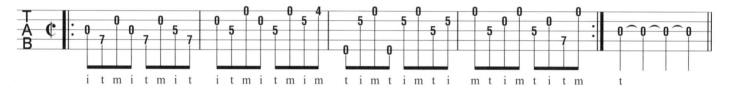

Fig. 108. Melodic Warmup Exercise No. 1

Melodic Exercise No. 2 (Fig. 109) has some letters written above the staff as well. These are the fingers I would suggest for fretting the notes.

▶ *Video 30*

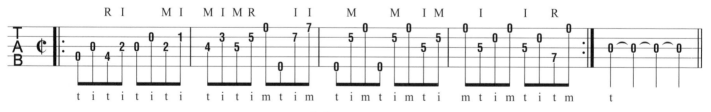

Fig. 109. Melodic Warmup Exercise No. 2

Melodic Exercise No. 3 (Fig. 110) is a little trickier. Notice that in measure 3, the 5th string is fretted on the 10th fret. To do this, wrap the thumb around and fret the string from the opposite side of the neck. Watch the video to see how this is done.

▶ *Video 31*

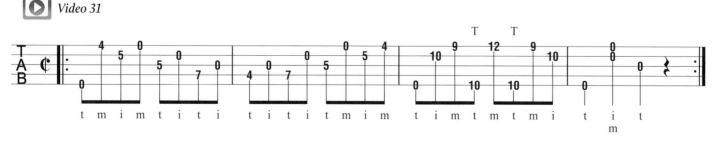

Fig. 110. Melodic Warmup Exercise No. 3

Let's play a few tunes in the melodic style.

Devil's Dream

"Devil's Dream" is an old Irish fiddle tune. It's also typically not in the key of G, so you would need to use a capo. The nice thing about this tune, in terms of learning the melodic style, is that it is fairly repetitive and not very complicated. Here are some things to look out for:

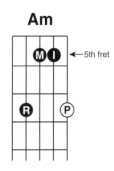

Am

← 5th fret

Fig. 111

- The first measure is mostly dealt with by the right hand; the only fretted note is the 1st string, 4th fret. I'd fret that with the ring finger.

- The first half of the second measure is identical, then we have a couple of fretted notes on the 5th fret of the 2nd and 3rd strings—using the index and middle fingers, respectively. For the next measure and a half, you are fretting a different form of the A minor (Am) chord. In Fig. 111, notice the white dot for the pinky finger shown on the 1st string. This note is optional. The full chord includes the pinky on the 1st string, 7th fret, but it is not needed in this song.

- Measures 5 and 6 are the same as measures 1 and 2, and then there's a little work for you to do in measures 7 and 8.

Learn this tune two measures at a time. When you get to the chorus, which starts at measure 9, you've learned everything you need to know from the first part, the verse.

First and Second Endings

There is a new concept to learn for this song: first and second endings. We've already discussed repeat signs. Sometimes, we use repeat signs together with first and second endings. In "Devil's Dream," we see a repeat sign at the end of measure 8. This tells you to go back to the beginning and repeat measures 1–8 as you normally would.

Now, notice the repeat signs at the end of measure 16 and the beginning of measure 9. When we get to the repeat sign at the end of measure 16, we jump back to measure 9 (not the beginning of the song) and play that section again. Notice the bracket above measures 15 and 16 with the "1" in the left corner; this is the *first ending*.

Here is what happens: You play all the way to the repeat sign, and then repeat measures 9–14. Then, when you get to the first ending again, skip over it this time and play the *second ending*.

In our example, the second ending is the end of the song, but if there were more to the song, we would play through the second ending and continue to the song's end.

In summary:

- Play measures 1–8.

- Repeat measures 1–8.

- Continue playing measures 9–16.

- Repeat measures 9–14.

- Jump to the second ending and play measures 17 and 18.

This tune is a very good exercise for the melodic style. There's a fair amount of repetition here, so it makes it a bit easier. The recording is in the key of A, using a capo on the 2nd fret (indicated with "Capo II" in the written music). We did this because A is a good key for the fiddle player. Finally, notice that the actual chords in the key of A are above the chords in the key of G, which are in parentheses.

DEVIL'S DREAM

Key of A
Capo II

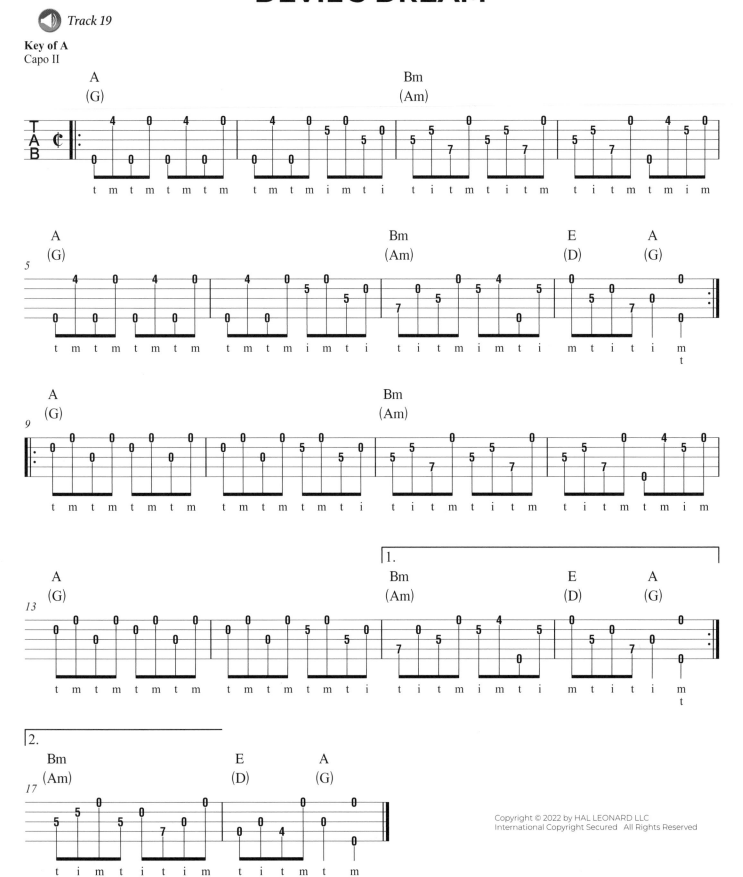

Soldier's Joy

"Soldier's Joy" is another good melodic exercise. This tune almost immediately breaks one of the rules established earlier. When first learning the right-hand rolls, we were warned against picking two notes in a row with the same finger—unless there was space between them, like a rest, or they were slower notes, like quarter notes. We also said there would be exceptions, and we have one here. At the beginning of measure 4, we have the same note played twice with the thumb—the 4th string, 7th fret.

SOLDIER'S JOY

Key of A
Capo II

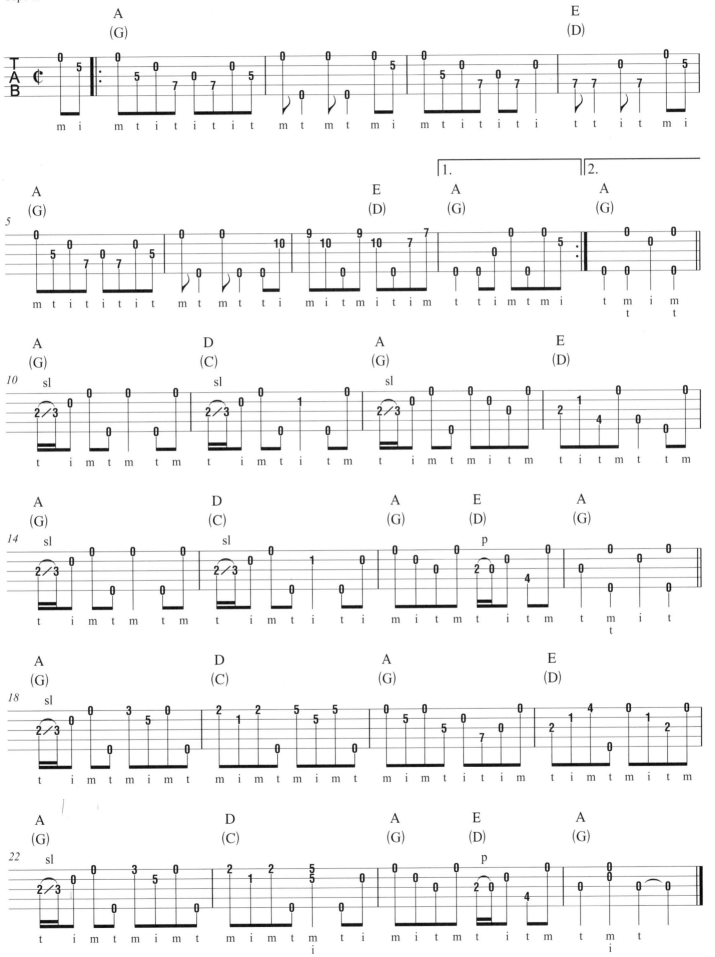

Double Banjo

Double banjo refers to just that: two banjos playing together. However, they're *not* playing the same thing; they're playing in *harmony*. Dictionary.com defines harmony as "the simultaneous combination of tones, especially when blended into chords pleasing to the ear." Based on the number of banjo jokes out there, we might get some varying opinions on just how pleasing the banjo actually *is* to the ear; but that's a matter of opinion and if you're reading this, I'm guessing we agree that it *is* pleasing. Anyway, in vocal or instrumental harmony, there's usually one voice singing or playing the melody and at least a second voice usually a *3rd* above. (A 3rd is the distance from scale degree 1 to scale degree 3, from scale degree 2 to scale degree 4, from scale degree 3 to scale degree 5, etc.) In this context, a "voice" could be a real voice or a note played on an instrument. There can be more voices forming the harmony, but we'll work with two.

The art of playing double banjo is especially impressive because of the complexity of what's going on. You have those melody notes, but they're surrounded by the rolls. That said, the first banjo is playing a pretty normal part, and it's up to the second banjo to not only harmonize the melody notes but all those fill-in notes, as well. The tighter you are playing together, the better it will sound.

In any written music, if there are multiple parts, there are multiple connected staffs: one for each part. Below, we have a *double staff*. The top of each pair is the first part, and the bottom is the second part. They are labeled "Banjo 1" and "Banjo 2." One player plays the lines labeled "Banjo 1," while the other simultaneously plays the lines labeled "Banjo 2." The example below is "Mary Had a Little Lamb." It's very simple, but it demonstrates the idea quite well.

MARY HAD A LITTLE LAMB

 Track 21

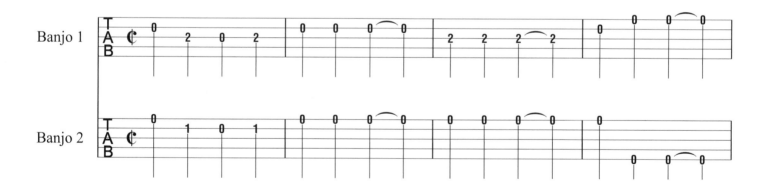

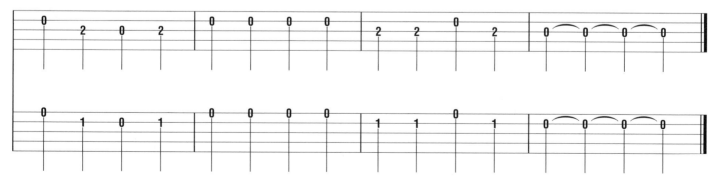

Earlier, we said that the bluegrass style of banjo approximates the melody and uses a lot of other chord tones to fill in. In a double banjo situation, the idea is to harmonize those melody notes, plus as many of the fill notes as possible. In addition, the closer the two players are rhythmically, the better. That means playing slides, pull-offs, and hammer-ons at the same time. The exercises here are very basic, but they will help to further demonstrate how banjo harmony works.

Here are a couple of examples of familiar licks, now played in harmony by two banjos.

Track 22

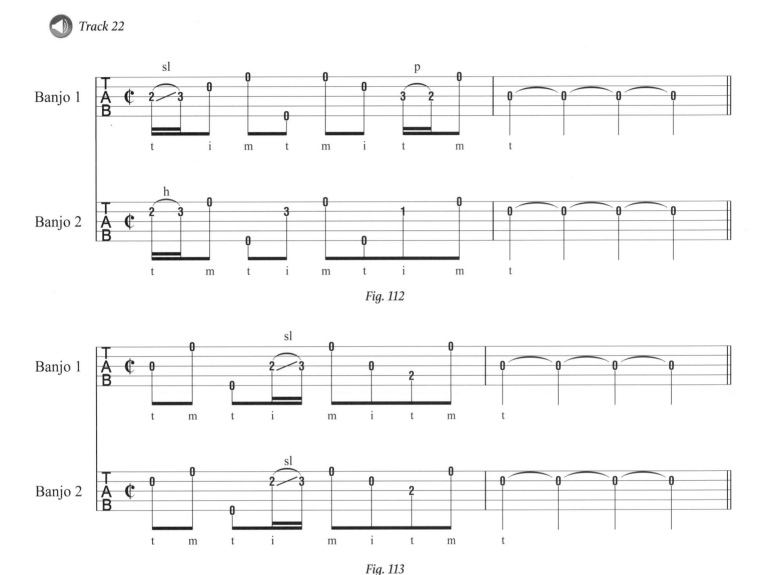

Fig. 112

Fig. 113

Old Joe Clark

Our first double banjo tune is "Old Joe Clark." The first part, the melody, stands up perfectly well on its own, so I suggest you learn it so you can play this tune whether or not there is a second banjo to play with. Once you learn the intricacies of the first part, you'll find that the harmony part is a simple matter of moving the left hand up to the proper frets and doing almost exactly the same thing as the first part, just five frets higher.

The audio for this song includes both banjo parts and a guitar accompaniment. There are also two follow-up tracks, Track 23b and Track 23c. These are the individual banjo parts, separated, so you can listen to one part while playing the other. Track 23b is the first banjo part only, allowing you to play the harmony, and Track 23c is the harmony, allowing you to play the melody.

"Old Joe Clark" is played in A, which again is simply capoed on the 2nd fret and played as you would in G. The fiddle and mandolin are much more comfortable in A on this one. If you're practicing it alone, it's totally up to you whether or not to use the capo.

OLD JOE CLARK

Capo II

Track 23b

Track 23c

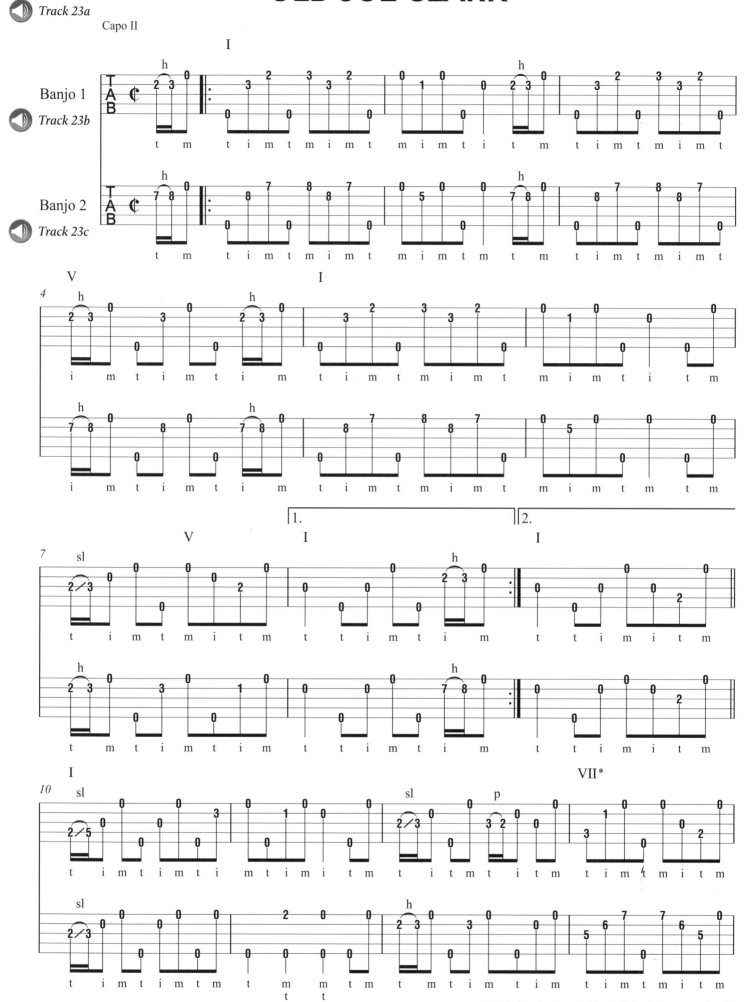

*This is actually outside of diatonic harmony, but in terms of the key of G, it would just be an F chord.

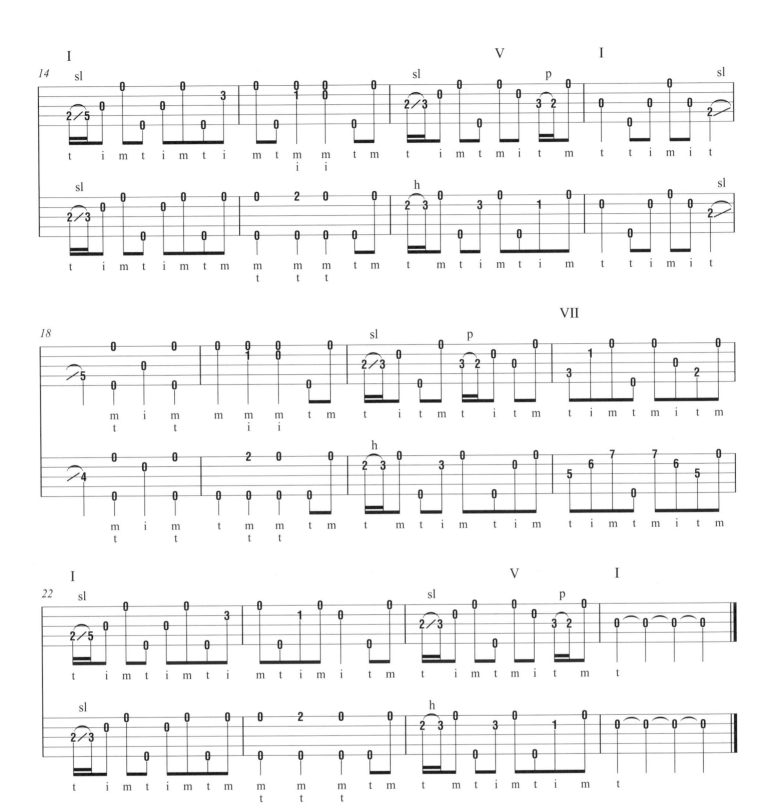

Big Ben

Another great double banjo tune, and one of my personal favorites, is "Big Ben." It's not a difficult song to play and it sounds great. There are several things to watch out for here. In the pickup measure and in measure 8, there are some eighth-note hammer-ons; make sure you're not doing those as sixteenth notes. Also, the second section—starting at measure 17—consists mainly of forward-backward rolls. Notice, however, that the last beat in measures 20, 24, and 28 is a quarter note. These brief pauses in the rhythm give you a moment to change chords. If you can play the complete roll and still make the chord change, by all means, include that last note; but if you make it a quarter note in one part, be sure to do it in the other part as well. A tight match is what double banjo is all about.

Track 24a includes both banjo parts and a guitar accompaniment. Track 24b is the first banjo part only, allowing you to play the harmony. Track 24c is the second banjo part—the harmony—allowing you to play the melody.

Again, this one is in the key of A, capoed on the 2nd fret.

BIG BEN

Words and Music by Ben Burchfield

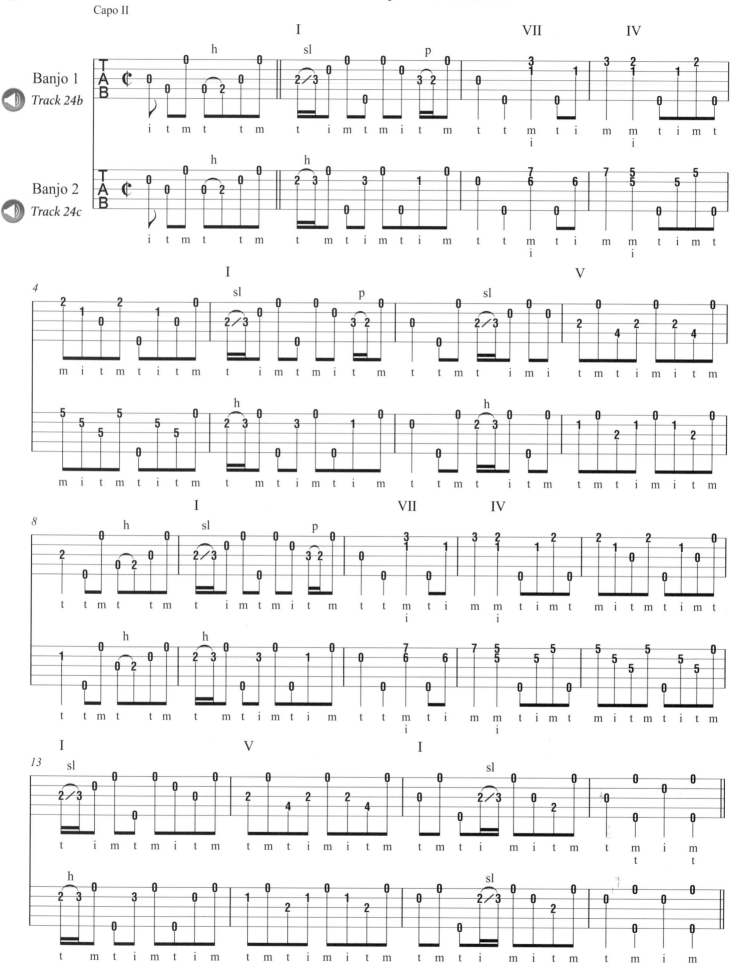

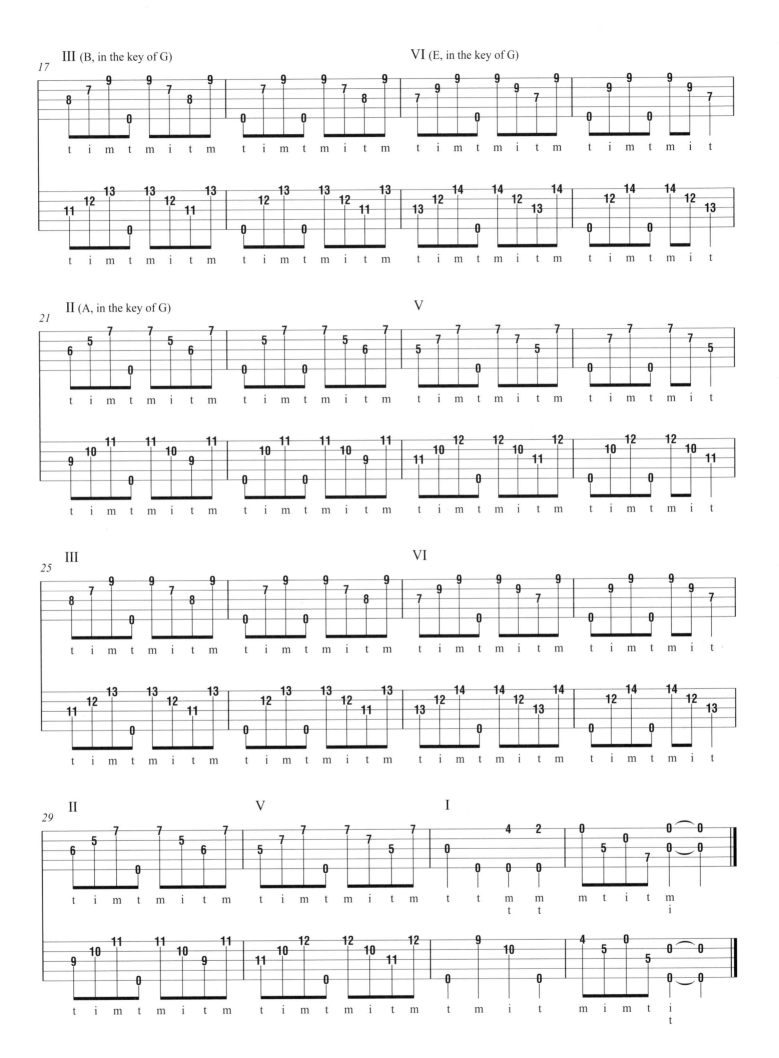

Playing in Different Keys

We mentioned in the Using the Capo chapter that the key of a tune is often decided by the comfortable range of the singer(s). That is usually solved by moving up or down a step. With a banjo, that is often achieved with a capo. If you know the tune in G and the singer would be more comfortable in A, simply put the capo on the 2nd fret and you're good to go. Don't forget the 5th-string capo.

However, we may also find that some songs are in keys we can handle without a capo. A good example is the key of C. The I, IV, and V chords in the key of C are C, F, and G. Because of the voicings of the chords, the sound differs from the open G position and gives some variety to your playing. There is no need to automatically use a capo. Then again, some C tunes sound better if you capo up to the 5th fret and play out of a G position. Listen to Bill Monroe's "Rawhide" for an example of this. Taking this a step further (literally), Doug Dillard recorded several tunes in the key of D in which he capoed on the 7th fret. It sounds great.

Let's try a quick exercise in C, then a full tune.

 Track 25

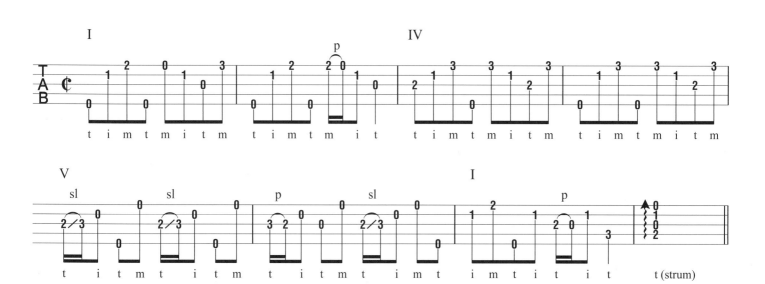

Fig. 114

Seeing Nellie Home (Aunt Dinah's Quilting Party)

Here's a fun tune played in C position. On the recording, it's capoed at the 2nd fret, making it the key of D. We did it this way because most of the available recordings of this song are in D—probably for the benefit of the fiddle. Remember though, you can first learn it without the capo, then put the capo on and play along with the recording. There are two breaks, meaning it goes through the solo twice; the first is a bit easier and the second is a little more challenging. Remember, once you learn them, you are free to take what you like from either break to mix and match into another version.

Here are a few things to notice:

- Measure 4 is a C7-position chord, which is a C with the pinky finger added to the 3rd fret of the 3rd string. This is optional, so if it's difficult at first, you can leave that string open. However, the last two notes of that measure should be played as written because they allow you to change to the F position for the IV chord. Hint: When changing from the C to the F, don't lift the index finger. It is in the same place for both chords!

- This is not written in the tab, but you may notice on the recording that the beginning of measure 5 is actually a hammer-on from the open 3rd string to the 2nd fret. This is optional.

- The strum at the end of the tune takes place on beat 3 of the measure. It's a C-position chord, but notice that there is a hammer-on from the open 1st string to the 2nd fret.

[song starts on the next page to allow for easier reading]

SEEING NELLIE HOME
(Aunt Dinah's Quilting Party)
Words by J. Fletcher
Music by Francer Kyle

 Track 26

Key of D
(C position)
Capo II

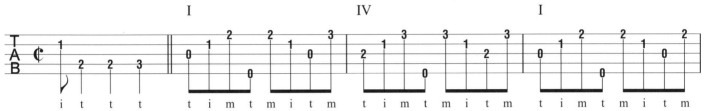

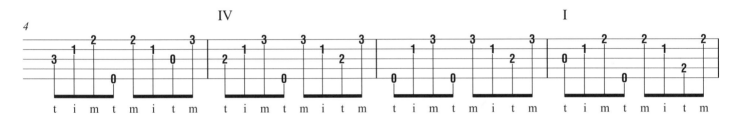

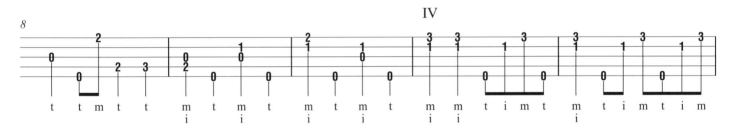

2nd Break

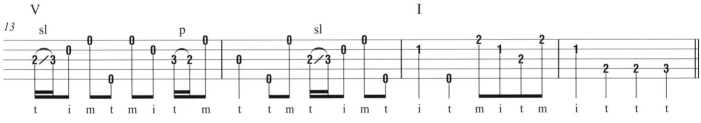

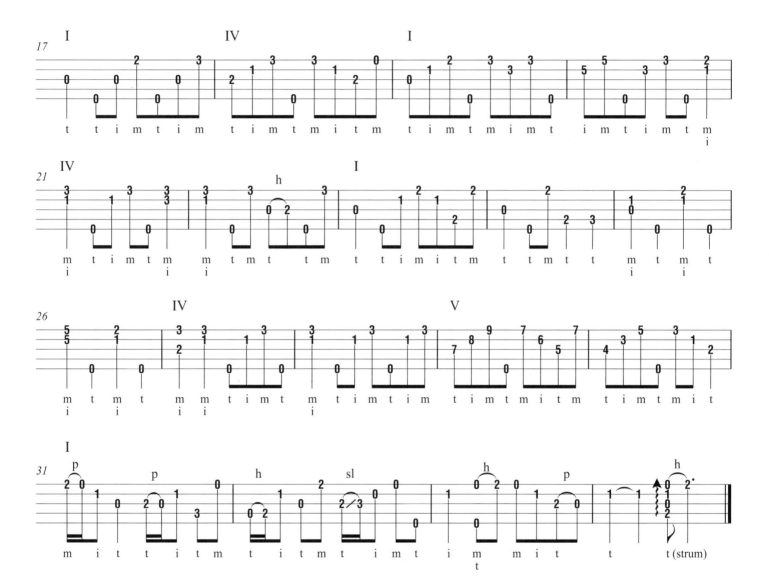

In Despair

This tune is played in the C position. A lot of bands play this in D, so let's capo up to the 2nd fret and play as though we're still in C.

IN DESPAIR

Words and Music by Joe Ahr and Juanita Pennington

 Track 27

Key of D
(C position)
Capo II

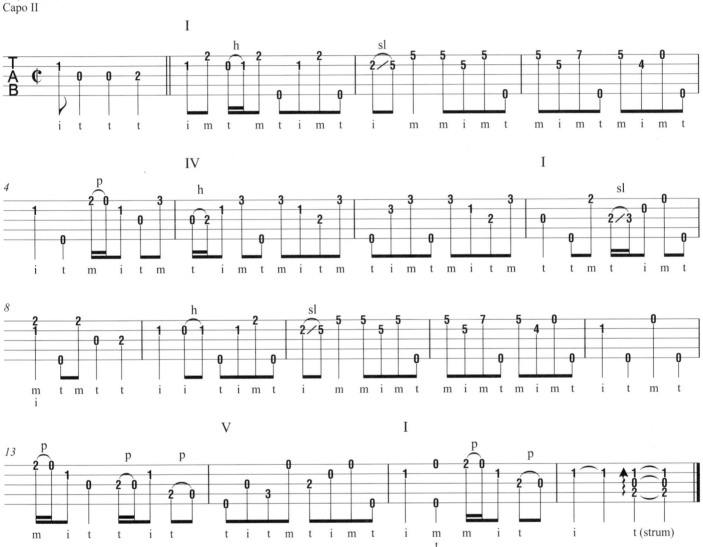

There Is a Time

Here is a good example of two different concepts:

- Playing in other keys
- The major vs. minor sound

This tune is in the key of E minor. According to the rules, E minor (Em) is the i chord, so, the iv and v chords are Am and Bm. In a minor key, iv and v are minor as well as the i. Remember, lowercase Roman numerals are used to indicate minor chords.

In the last measure, notice the symbol above the second beat. This is a *fermata*, and it tells you to hold that chord longer than the written value.

No capo is needed for this one.

THERE IS A TIME
Words by Mitchell F. Jayne
Music by Rodney Dillard

Track 28

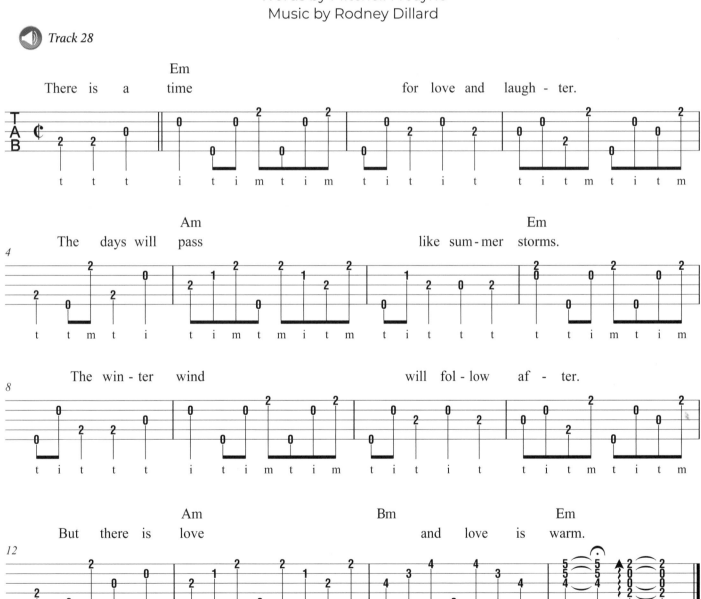

Tricks

D Tuners

There are several interesting tricks you can do on the banjo to make your performance a little flashier. For instance, there is a special kind of tuning peg known as a *D tuner*. The original D tuners could switch the banjo's tuning from open G to open D, hence the name. However, they have been improved upon and can do much more than that now. They are commonly used on the 2nd and 3rd strings, but some players will use them on the 1st and 4th, too. You might also hear these called "Scruggs" or "Keith" tuners, named after the banjo pioneers who invented and experimented with them.

Typically, this is your little secret. Nobody knows about them and suddenly, in the middle of a tune, you go for your tuners, while playing, and re-tune the banjo. Naturally, the crowd goes crazy.

Of course, the secret is that you can set an upper and a lower note on the tuner and lock it so it won't go any farther. You tune down until it stops, and back up until it stops. This is done with small thumb screws on the back of the tuner.

In tablature, we show this with an arrow and a "1" or "1/2" above it to indicate a whole-step or half-step change. We pick the string open, and then an arrow follows to show which direction to re-tune the string—up or down.

The most common tuning with tuners is from open G to open D. Here's how to do it:

1. Start by tuning your banjo normally.

2. Set the upper stops of your 2nd- and 3rd-string pegs (B and G, respectively).

3. Move the 2nd string down to A and set the lower stop.

4. Move the 3rd string down to F♯ and set the lower stop.

Here are a couple of hints. First, you may have to do this a few times: readjusting, re-tuning, and resetting the stops. Because of this, it's a good idea to start your set with one of these tunes so you're in tune and you're done with it. If you're in the middle of a set, you might need three or four minutes to set the pegs up.

Also, I like to take a conventional pencil and sharpen it. Then, loosen the 2nd and 3rd strings and pop them out of the slots in the nut. Draw in those slots with the pencil, getting a lot of graphite in there. This will keep the string moving freely, preventing it from snagging and going out of tune. (I keep a 0.3 mm mechanical pencil in my case for just this reason. If you use a mechanical pencil, you don't have to find a sharpener.)

Important Note:

- I would strongly suggest not using a capo when using the D-tuners. It can keep the strings from moving freely and might put you out of tune.

- Also, I would make a point of using fairly new strings. Older strings tend to stretch more, and again, might go out of tune when using the D-tuners.

Flint Hill Special

Following is the first break of "Flint Hill Special," probably the best-known D-tuner song. Overall, it's a combination of pretty standard bluegrass licks, but the chorus is heavy on the tuners. The opening line—first four measures—is banjo only, so the chord symbols don't appear until the second line when the accompaniment starts. (Note: The written music has rests, but you can let the notes that precede them ring through these. This is actually done quite often in banjo music.)

[song starts on the next page to allow for easier reading]

FLINT HILL SPECIAL

By Earl Scruggs

 Track 29

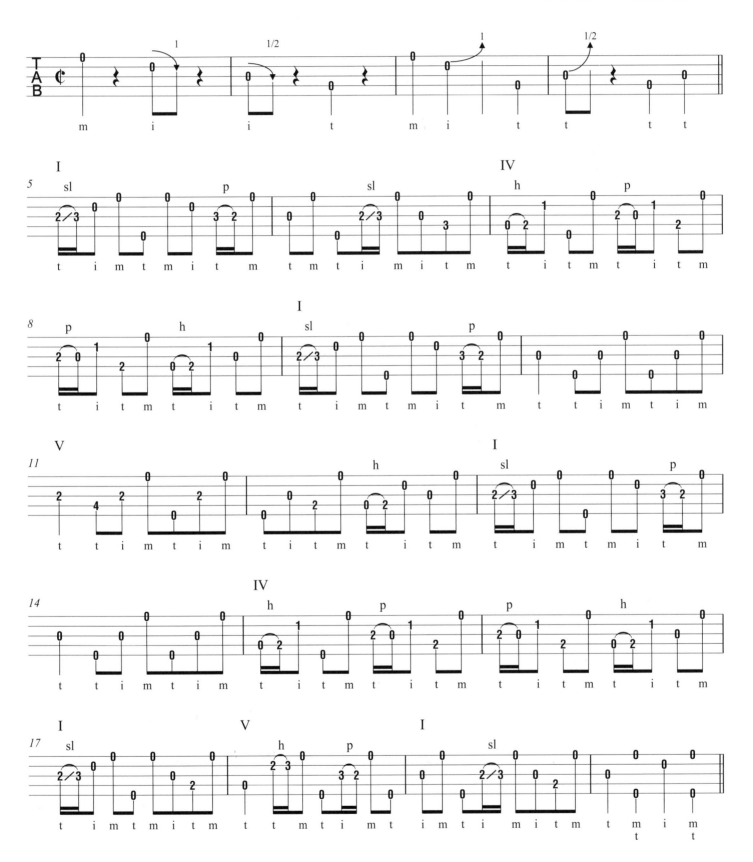

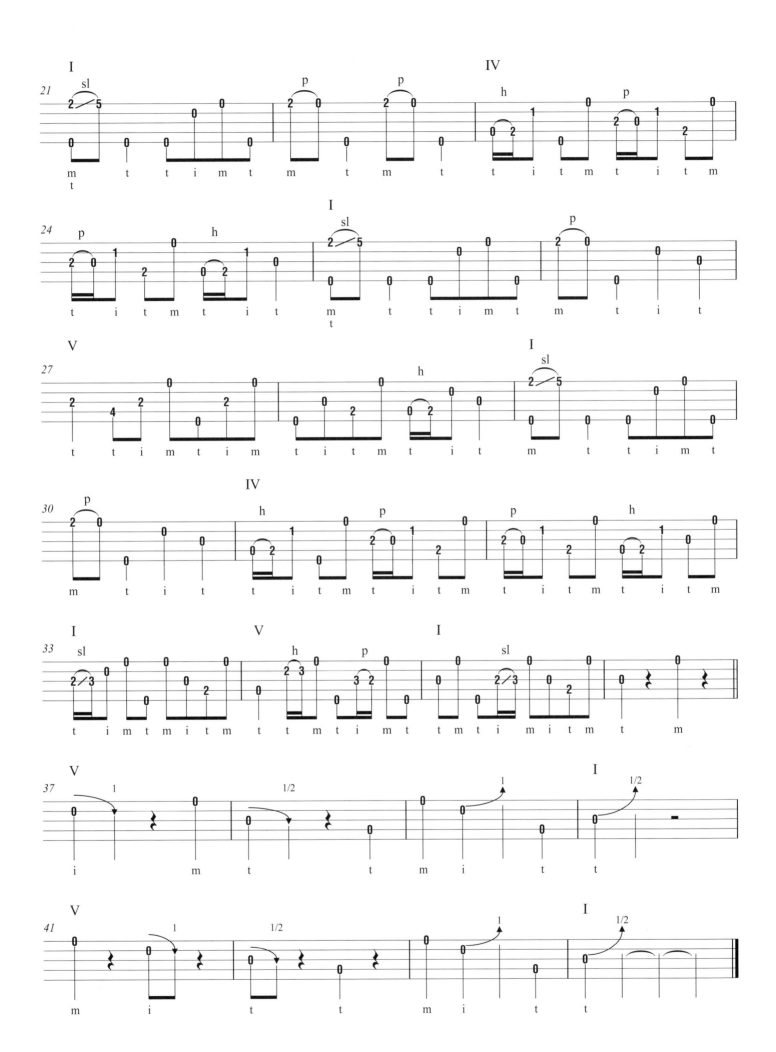

Harmonics/Chimes

Harmonics, or *chimes*, are easy to play (though maybe not to understand). Let's get a little into physics here. A string produces sound when it vibrates. The string is supported at each end by the bridge and the nut. The string does not vibrate at these two points. Imagine the length of the string as a bit of an arc, vibrating at its widest in the middle and not at all at the ends. This is the first of the four images in Fig. 115.

If you divide the length of the string in half and touch it lightly, that arc will split into two arcs, each being one-half the length of the string. The string will not vibrate at this midpoint, or *node*. On a 5-string banjo, this node is directly over the 12th fret. Done correctly, you will get a tone one octave higher than the open string. If you play the 3rd string G, you'll get a high G. This is the second of the four images in Fig. 115.

If you divide the length of the string into thirds and touch it lightly (over the 7th fret), the string will split into three arcs, each being one-third the length of the string. You will get a note an octave and a 5th above the open string. Doing this on the open G string will produce a high D. This is the third of the four images in Fig. 115.

This continues. The spot over the 5th fret is one-fourth the string length, where you'll get a note two octaves higher than the open string. These harmonics, also called the *overtone series*, continue, but they get progressively difficult to play and hear.

▶ *Video 32*

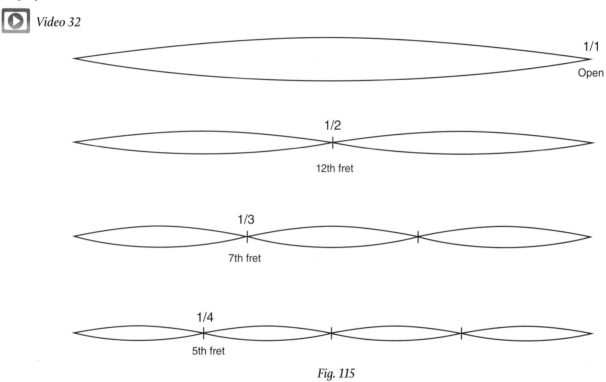

Fig. 115

To play the harmonic, touch the string very lightly *directly over* the proper fret. Don't push it down as you normally would when fretting a note. Pick it and lift the finger off the string. It will continue to sound. See Video 23 for a demonstration.

In tablature, a harmonic is indicated by the abbreviation "Harm." above the fret number. In Fig. 116, we see individual 12th-fret harmonics on the 3rd, 2nd, and 1st strings; then, we have a couple of chords on the first three strings at the 7th and 5th frets.

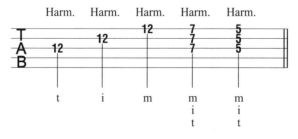

Fig. 116

Foggy Mountain Chimes

It's time for a song. Earlier, in "Flint Hill Special," we talked about the D tuners. In this next tune, "Foggy Mountain Chimes," we use the tuners, but we're including harmonics as well.

Here are a couple of quick tips:

- Be ready for the count-off in the audio; you only get two beats.

- In measure 8, your index finger is already on the 3rd string, 2nd fret. Leave it there when you move to measure 9, and just do the slide with the index finger. That's not the usual way, but why lift it and replace it with another finger?

- Once you tune down in measures 18 and 19, leave it there until the final two measures, after the 2nd ending.

[song starts on the next page to allow for easier reading]

FOGGY MOUNTAIN CHIMES

By Earl Scruggs

 Track 30

G and D Tunings
G: (5th-1st) G-D-G-B-D
D: (5th-1st) G-D-F#-A-D

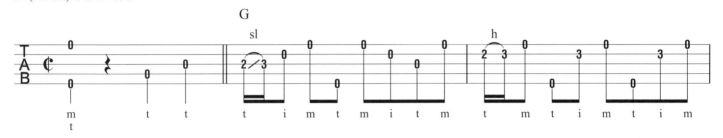

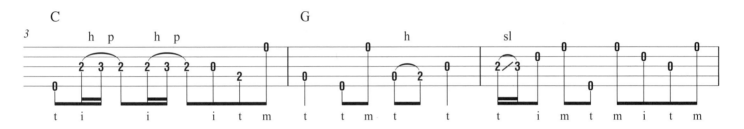

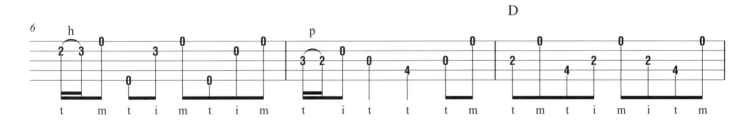

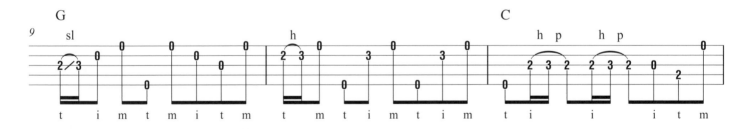

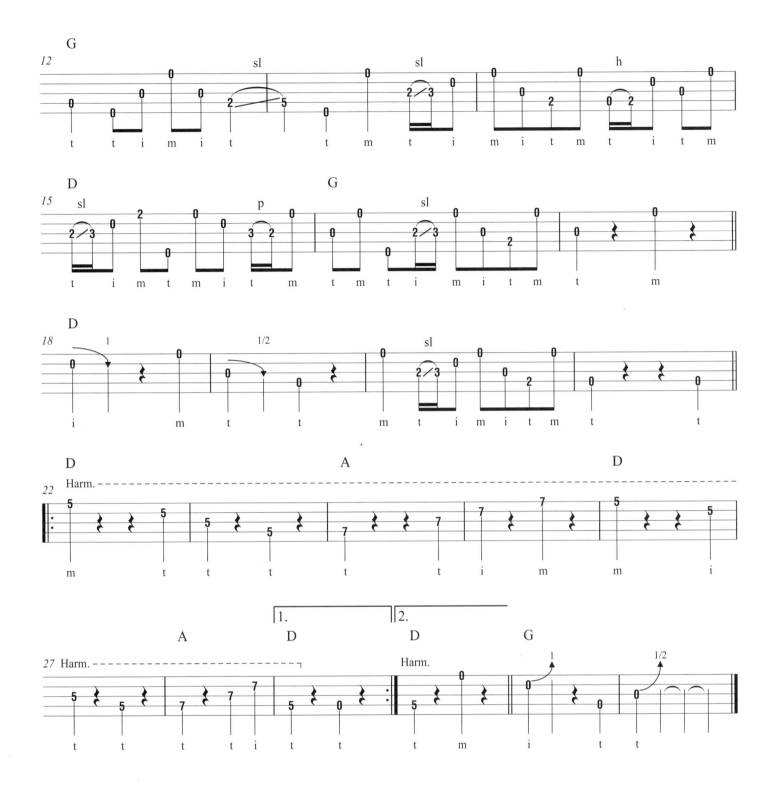

Chokes (Bends)

The choke is a classic sound associated with bluegrass banjo. It can be incorporated into a lead solo as well as back-up. It's a simple matter of bending an already-fretted string, changing its pitch by a half or whole step. The most common example is done on the 10th fret of the 2nd string. Notice in the examples below that there is a curved line after the notes to be choked.

For this example:

- Start with Roll No. 6. Play it a few times to refresh your memory. Don't forget to bring the thumb up to the 2nd string. Play the roll several times and end it with the single note on the 2nd string.

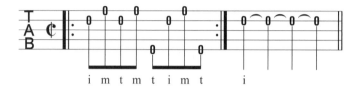

- Next, fret the 2nd string on the 10th fret and play it again several times. In this form, end it on the 2nd string, 8th fret.

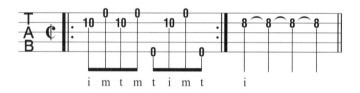

- Finally, when picking the fretted string (in this case, the 2nd string), push it upward to change the pitch. Again, this is indicated by the curved line adjacent to the choked notes. This is done each time, so after picking it the first time, move back to the normal fretted position and bend it again. When finished, end it on the 2nd string, 8th fret.

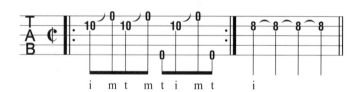

Tag Licks

We have mentioned that a phrase in music is much like a phrase in a sentence; it's creates a natural pause point. Musically, a logical phrase might be one line in the lyrics. If it's an instrumental tune, it might be a certain number of measures, like four or eight. As you get used to playing, you'll be able to feel where phrases begin and end. The end of a phrase might use a tag lick like the one shown in Fig. 117.

Track 31

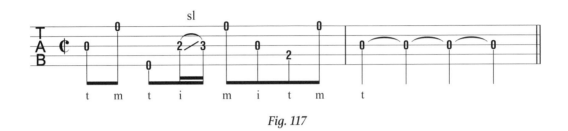

Fig. 117

In context, a phrase might appear as eight measures with chord changes like I–IV–I–V and back to I, possibly two measures each. As we get toward the end of the phrase, we see the V chord, leading to the I. At this point, when there are vocals, there's a pause in the lyrics. In an instrumental, it might be the end of one instrument's solo (break), leading to the next.

The next four examples are tags that the banjo might play in such a situation. A tag has a sound of finality, like a period in a sentence. A tag can be used at the end of a tune, but it can also be used at the end of a phrase or section.

Track 32

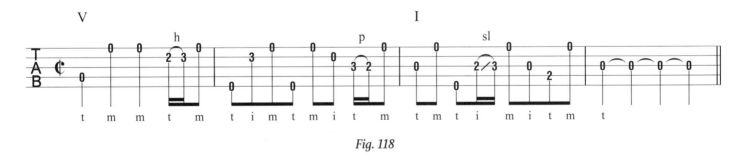

Fig. 118

Track 33

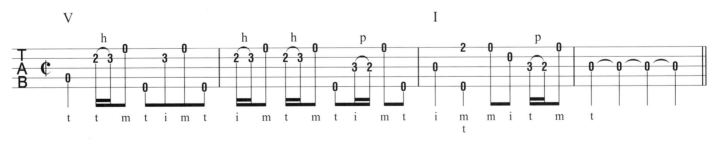

Fig. 119

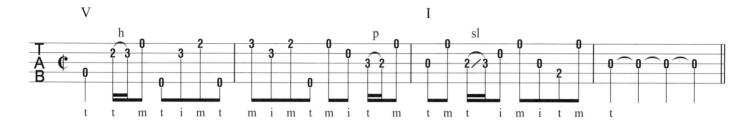

Fig. 120

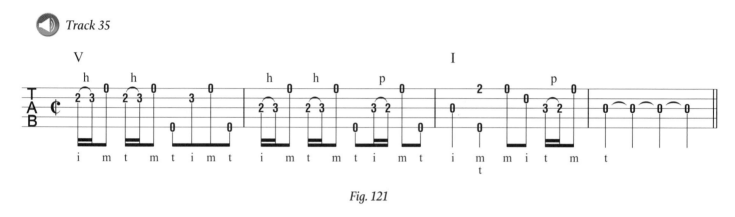 *Track 35*

Fig. 121

You can take the first two measures from any one of the previous four examples (Figs. 118–121) and combine it with the last two measures from any other of the four examples. Try it. Mix and match! Put them together, and you'll see they work great.

TOOLBOX

Use a Metronome!

A tried-and-true way of honing both your rhythm and speed on any instrument is by practicing with a *metronome*, which is a simple device that produces a steady, regular click sound, usually in beats per minute (BPM). These days, you can find metronome apps online, often for free.

Carefully playing along to a metronome's click forces you to play in steady rhythm; doing this consistently over time will surely sharpen your timing. Another great benefit of metronome use is to help build your speed. Start at the slowest speed you can comfortably play the song or practice material you are working on and gradually increase the click speed in small increments. Do this until you've reached the fastest you can play. Continue this regimen every practice session and you're guaranteed to see results!

Endings

It's often up to the banjo to end a tune. The type of ending depends on the song. It can be simple, like the one shown in Fig. 122, or more complex. This one can be tacked on right after the last notes of the final chorus or solo, and it's a nice quick ending.

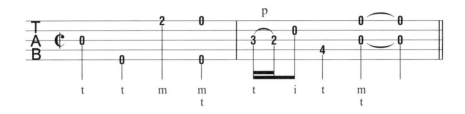

Fig. 122

Or, we can get a bit more involved... fancier. Following is a set of standard mix-and-match endings. By mix and match, we mean that a lot of endings of this type have a first half (a setup) and a second half (a conclusion). You may have heard the phrase "shave and a haircut." The rhythm of the second half corresponds to the syllables of the words "shave and a haircut, two bits."

On the following page, we have an A part (the first two measures) and a B part (the second two measures). If you simply play across the pages, the A and B parts will match up just fine. But, you can take any A part and match it up with any B part, and you'll have another ending. Some work together better than others, but that's for you to decide. A large part of bluegrass playing is to learn lots of licks, and then put them together in effective combinations. This is as true for endings as it is for any other parts of a tune.

In examples 1, 2, and 3 in the B parts, notice the final two notes ("two bits") are played on either the 1st string or the 5th. Personally, I tend to use the 5th string, picked with the thumb, but the notes are on the same frets whether you use the 1st or 5th string. It's up to you to choose which works better for you.

Finally, example 6 is more melodic, and I reserve this type of ending for a fiddle tune. The first three notes are a *triplet*, which fits three eighth notes evenly into the time used for two eighth notes. Listen to the audio track for help with this one.

Part A

Track 36

1.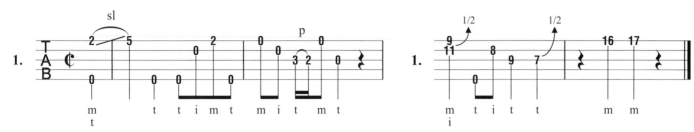

Track 37

2.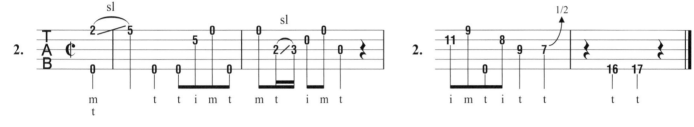

Track 38

3.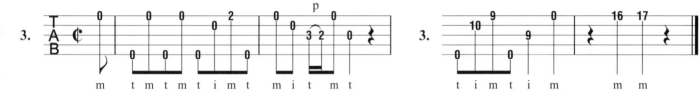

Track 39

4.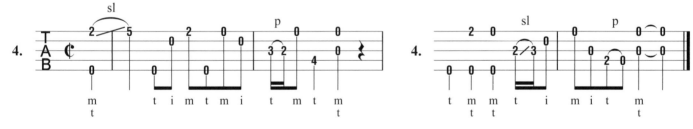

Track 40

5.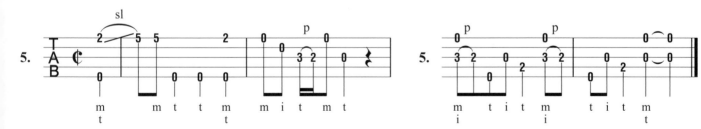

Track 41

6.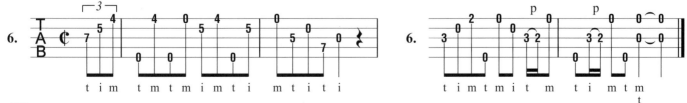

Part B

1.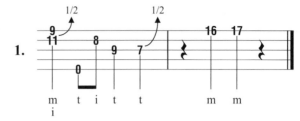

2.

3.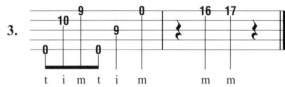

4.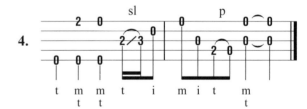

5.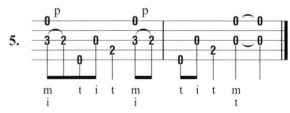

6.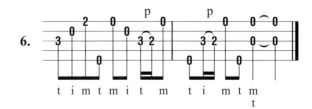

Maintenance

Changing Strings

It's going to happen. It's just a matter of time before you're sitting around, playing with friends or playing a gig, and all of a sudden you hear a loud "pop." You busted a string. Fear not, with a little practice, you can replace a single string in as little as a minute.

Naturally, you need to be prepared. Never be without at least one extra set of strings. If, over time, you find that you consistently break a certain string, you can buy singles; have a few extras of the problem strings in your case.

I also keep a small wire cutter in my case, but you can get away without one.

A 5-string banjo normally uses steel loop-end strings. This means that one end of the string is twisted around with a loop (see Fig. 123). The tailpiece on the banjo has hooks or knobs that the loop goes over, and that holds the string in place. The opposite end of the string goes over the bridge, over the nut, and through a hole in the shaft of the appropriate tuning peg.

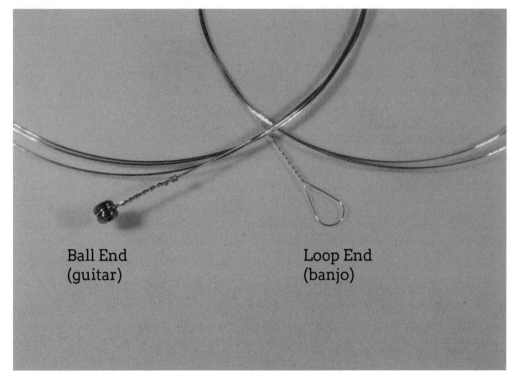

Fig. 123

Start by checking the path of the old strings. They start on the hook on the tailpiece and go through or under parts of the tailpiece. Keep that path in mind when installing the new string.

Whether I'm replacing one string or the full set, I usually do it one at a time. The strings hold the bridge in place, so if you take them all off at once, you also have to deal with getting the bridge back in the right place. This isn't a major operation, but by changing the strings one at a time, you won't have to deal with it at all. The following section, Adjusting the Bridge, shows you how to do this in case you need to.

 Video 33

1. Remove any remnants of the old string and get the new string unwrapped and straightened out.

2. Place the loop end over the hook or knob on the tailpiece and run it through the proper path. From there, it goes over the bridge and over the nut.

3. This is important! Thread the end of the string through the hole in the tuning peg. It is important that the strings come up between the pegs and wrap around from the center of the peghead outward (see Fig. 124).

4. Don't pull the string tight. Leave enough slack so you have to turn the peg at least five or six full revolutions before the string is in tune. That keeps it from slipping. Except for the 4th string, which is wound, the strings are very smooth; if one isn't on correctly, it will slip out of tune or even come right off when you start putting pressure on it by playing.

5. When I start to wrap the string, I let the end pass below the main portion of the string on the first revolution, then, for the rest of it, I let the end pass *over* it. It's not exactly a knot, but it seems to hold a little better.

Fig. 124

Please watch Video 33. It is much easier to understand the process by watching a demonstration than it is to just read the description. Note that in the video, we don't discuss the tailpiece. There are many different types of tailpieces, so I suggest looking closely at yours before removing the old string to see how it passes through.

Adjusting the Bridge

Bridge position is critical, and because a banjo bridge is held in place only by the strings, it can move. If it moves, you will have intonation problems. The operational part of the string, as we know, is between the nut and the bridge. The halfway point is the 12th fret. If the bridge is moved slightly toward the nut, your fretted notes will be sharp—slightly high; if the bridge is moved slightly toward the tailpiece, your fretted notes will be flat—slightly low. The bridge should also be perpendicular to the strings. There is some debate over this because as you use higher frets, the strings are a bit higher off the neck and sometimes tend to go sharp anyway, but that's a whole other discussion.

To check your bridge position, you really only need a tuner or a good ear.

1. Start by tuning the banjo to the tuner.

2. Play the 12th-fret harmonic of the 3rd string, checking to see that it is perfectly in tune. Be sure also that your finger is directly over the 12th fret when doing the harmonic.

3. Now, fret the 12th fret of the 3rd string and check to see whether it is also perfectly in tune. If it's slightly sharp/high, move the bridge slightly toward the tailpiece. If it's slightly flat/low, move the bridge slightly toward the nut or peghead.

Once it's in tune at the 12th fret, check the other strings. Make sure they are in tune when played open, then check the harmonic, then the 12th fret. Small adjustments may be required. When they're all good, you might take a pencil and draw a light outline around the feet of the bridge for reference.

There are several videos on the internet about adjusting the bridge. I'd recommend taking a look at those before starting.

Head Adjustment

This is an important adjustment, but it is also potentially problematic. It isn't difficult to overtighten and break the banjo head, so if you decide to do it yourself, be very conservative with your adjustments. There are lots of videos on YouTube that can help you with this.

The vibrations created by playing the banjo can cause parts to loosen up over time. If you see that the bridge is pushing the head down or if you can change the pitch of the strings by squeezing the head, it's too loose. To make the adjustment, you need a couple of basic tools:

- A nut driver
- A tuner

Remove the resonator—the rear part of the body. In most cases, it's held on by four larger thumb screws. This will expose the hex nuts on the back of the hooks or brackets. A lot of this is done by feel. First of all, if the nut is very loose, turn it just until it starts to "grab" or until it is no longer spinning freely. From there, you can actually feel when all the nuts are similarly tight.

Some people prefer to start at one spot and just move clockwise from one nut to the next and give each one a slight turn—as little as 1/8 of a turn! I prefer to do one nut, then the one opposite from it. What I mean is, as you're looking at the brackets, tighten one, then go straight across to the one on the opposite side and adjust it next.

- However your banjo is positioned, start with the one in the top, 12 o'clock, position.
- Then, move to the bottom 6 o'clock position.
- From there, go to 3 o'clock, then 9 o'clock, and continue until all are tightened.

Changing the Banjo Head

It is critical that you turn each nut only a quarter turn or so each time. It is better to err in favor of too loose than too tight. One Saturday morning a few years ago, about four hours before a date in the recording studio, I decided to tighten my head, when suddenly I heard a sickening "pop" sound. In the entire city, I could find only one banjo head, and it wasn't the type I usually use. It gave my banjo a whole different sound. Now, whenever I hear that record, all I hear is that banjo head. Not only that, but it created an emergency. I had to get to town, buy and change the head, and get it all up and running in time for the session. I suggest tightening the head way before any performance, so that if something goes wrong, it won't become an emergency. Since that happened to me, I always have a new backup head on hand.

When you're satisfied that the tension is relatively good, replace the resonator and take a listen.

Again, there are several videos on the internet that can help you with this, some produced by banjo companies. I'd recommend taking a look at these before starting.

Appendix A:
Full Banjo Tunes

Now for some complete tunes! The following are previews from the *Hal Leonard Banjo Play-Along* series.

Each tune consists of two banjo breaks. The first is fairly basic, and the second is a bit more challenging. In addition, there's a mandolin part between the breaks where you can practice your backup playing.

There are two audio tracks provided for each tune: a Demo track with the full band, so you can hear what it should sound like; and a Play-Along track with the banjo part removed, so you can play along with the rest of the band.

Performance notes are also included here—introductory comments about each tune with information about some of the details and how to handle them.

Finally, some of the recordings are in different keys, using a capo. Just remember that, even if you don't have a capo yet, you can still learn them as written. Later, when you have a capo, you can get yourself in the right key to "play along."

> As of this writing, there are eight books in the *Hal Leonard Banjo Play-Along* series, each containing eight tunes. All books contain the same types of audio recordings, with a Demo and Play-Along track for each tune. To see and order these books, go to **www.halleonard.com** and search "Banjo Play Along."

Performance Notes

Will the Circle Be Unbroken
From Hal Leonard Banjo Play-Along Vol. 6, Songs for Beginners
The first break is pretty basic and shouldn't have any surprises. Notice that the upbeats in the backup to the mandolin break are the higher-position chords, starting with the D-position G chord on the 7th fret. The C and D chords in the backup are the F-position shapes. The backup is a suggestion; you can play anything you would like. Also, when playing along, there are two banjo breaks, but you can play the same one twice if you'd like. If you haven't yet learned the second break, play the first break both times... or make one up!

Black Mountain Rag
From Hal Leonard Banjo Play-Along Vol. 6, Songs for Beginners
One of my favorites, this is the first tune I learned by ear off of a recording. A well-known fiddle tune, this one is normally played in the key of A (capo 2nd fret), but is presented here in G. The first tricky section happens when the first C chord appears (measures 11–13). For the hammer-on on the 2nd string, hammer from the index to the middle finger. Leave the middle finger down on the 3rd fret, then use the index for the 2nd fret of the 1st string, and the ring for the 3rd fret. As you add each finger, leave the previous one down because you will be backing out of that position, one finger at a time.

In the second break, you'll be doing this again (measures 51–53) and adding a pull-off. There's a D chord at measures 55 and 56. Because of the melody here, you will be using a D7 chord. In the first measure of this chord (measure 55), start with that D7 position. For the second beat of this measure, keep the index finger down and use the ring finger for the 4th fret of the 4th string. In the next measure, keeping the index in place, use the middle finger for the 2nd fret of the 4th string. Lastly, for the final C chord (measure 59), start by fretting the 5th fret of the 3rd string with the middle finger. When it's time to fret the 2nd string, 5th fret, use the ring finger. Plus, on the right (picking) hand, you're just alternating between thumb and index. It's much easier than it looks or sounds.

The Red Haired Boy

From *Hal Leonard Banjo Play-Along Vol. 8, Celtic Bluegrass*

A combination of Scruggs-style and melodic, both banjo breaks switch freely between the styles, making this a very cool tune to play. In the chorus of the second banjo break, notice that the rest of the band plays drones on the D (I) chord in the first half, then resumes the regular progression in the second half. Here's another possibility: You can play every break like this, or just the last one—your choice.

In the second banjo break, specifically in measure 62, is a series of pull-offs out of an F position. The first half of the measure includes a pull-off on the 2nd string, followed in the second half by a pull-off on the 3rd string. After the first pull-off, be sure to put the index finger back down, because you're still in that F position and it needs to be fretted properly. On the second pull-off, it's not necessary because you're going back to the G (or I) chord.

Eighth of January

From *Hal Leonard Banjo Play-Along Vol. 9, Festival Favorites*

This tune is presented in two keys. Being a fiddle tune, the keys of A and D are both common. Because we're using a capo, they're both in G position for us; it's just the capo that has changed. Not many banjo players capo on the 7th fret for the key of D, but it's a great sound. Don't overuse it, but for tunes like this, "Soldier's Joy," "Liberty," and others, it sounds really nice.

That said, the first banjo break is in A. At the end of that break, it immediately changes to the key of D at measure 17, where the banjo begins playing backup for the mandolin (still capoed on the 2nd fret). The second banjo break begins with the pickups to measure 33, capoed on the 7th fret. Here, we can pause the recording, change the capo, tune it up, etc. In a real performance situation, it might not be that easy, so keep in mind that this is mainly for demonstration of the two keys. If you play it with a band, odds are that you'll either play it through in one key or you'll go back and forth between instruments, so having to change your capo is very unlikely. Notice also that the second banjo break repeats through twice. The final break starts with the pickups to measure 43, for a total of three breaks in this arrangement.

WILL THE CIRCLE BE UNBROKEN

Words by Ada R. Habershon
Music by Charles H. Gabriel

Track 42a - Demo

Track 42b - Play-Along

Key of G

G tuning:
(5th-1st) G-D-G-B-D

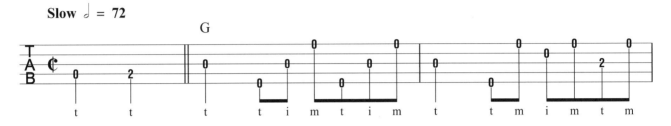

A Banjo Break

Slow ♩ = 72

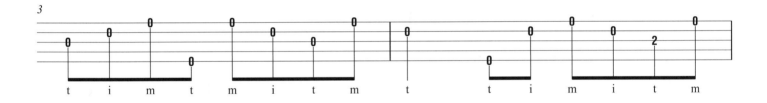

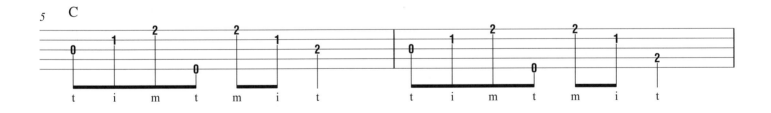

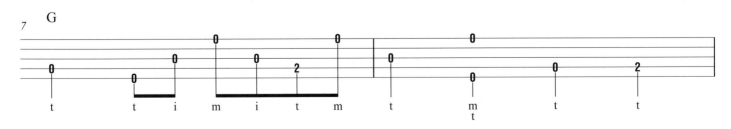

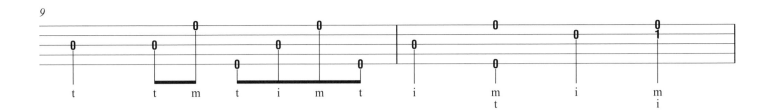

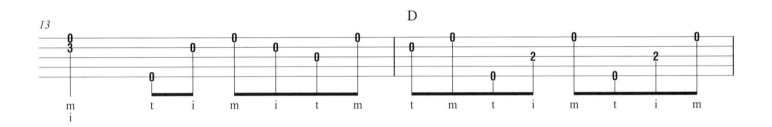

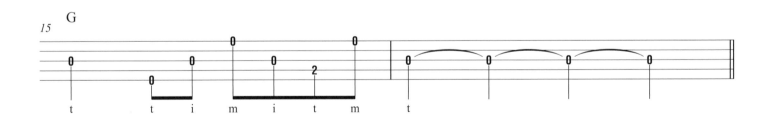

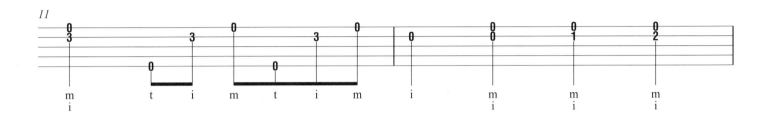

B **Mandolin Break**

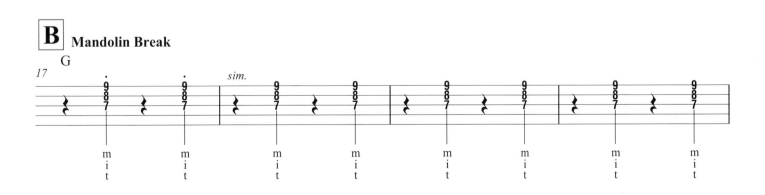

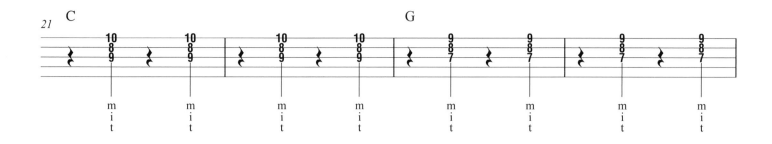

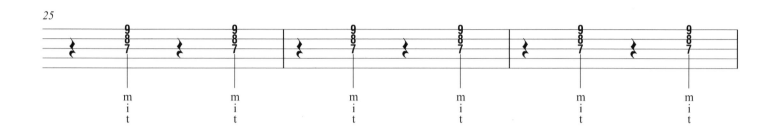

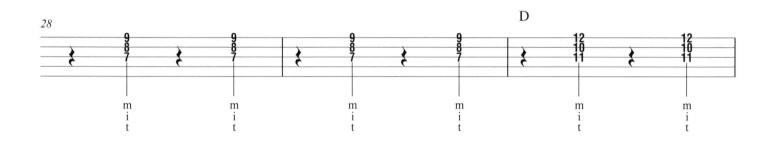

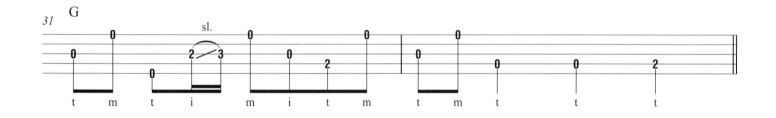

C Banjo Break

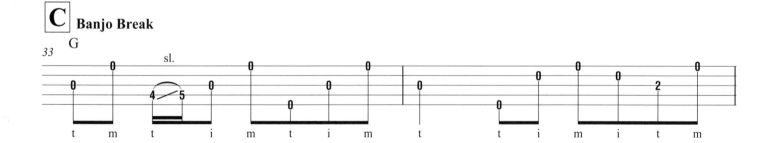

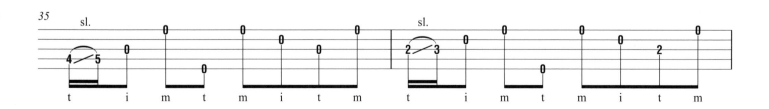

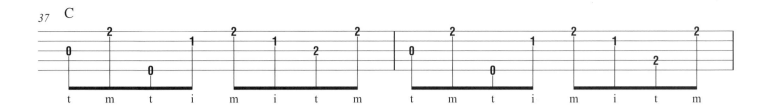

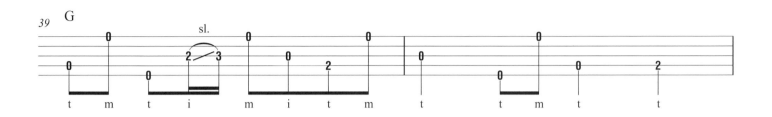

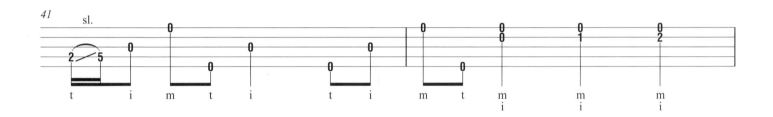

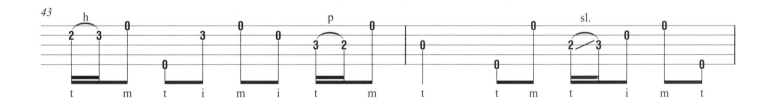

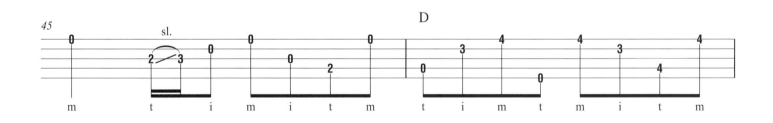

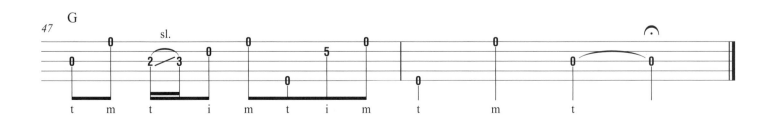

BLACK MOUNTAIN RAG

Traditional

Track 43a - Demo

Track 43b - Play-Along

Key of G

G tuning:
(5th-1st) G-D-G-B-D

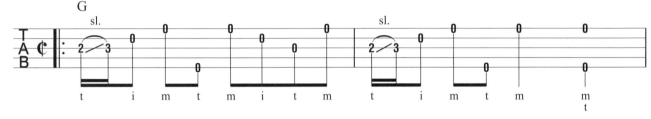

A **Banjo Break**

Slow ♩ = 56

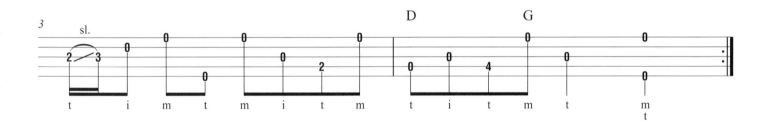

B

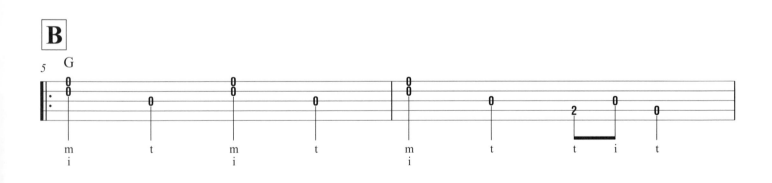

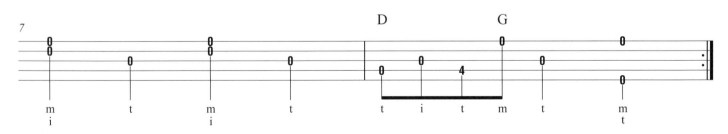

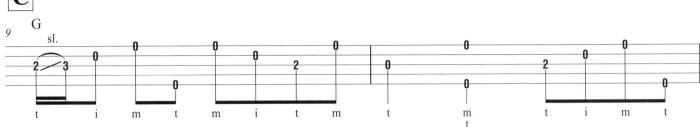

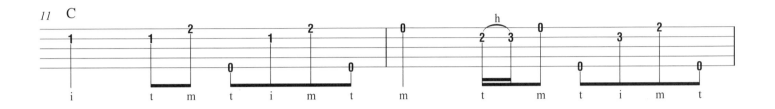

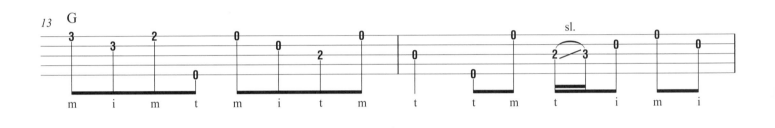

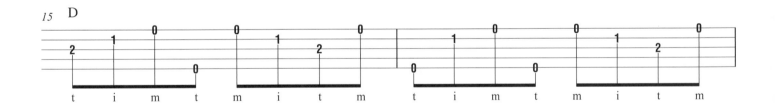

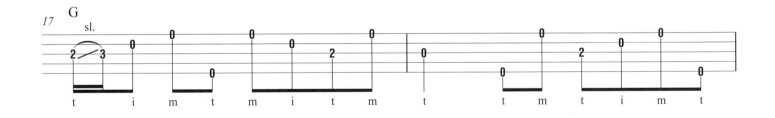

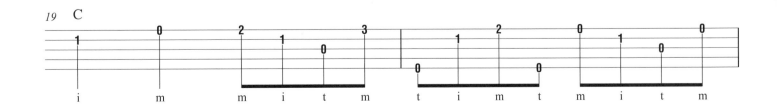

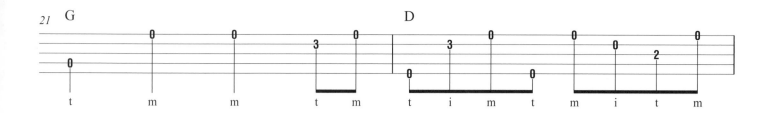

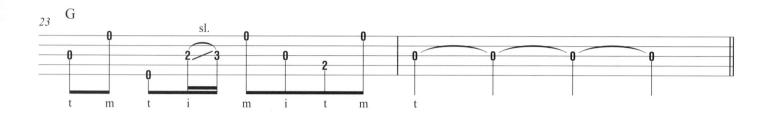

D Mandolin Break

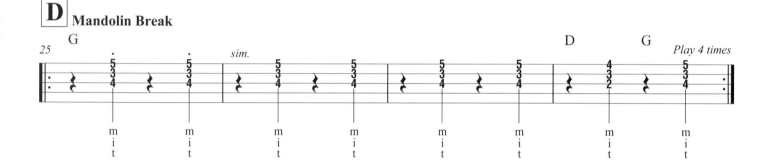

E

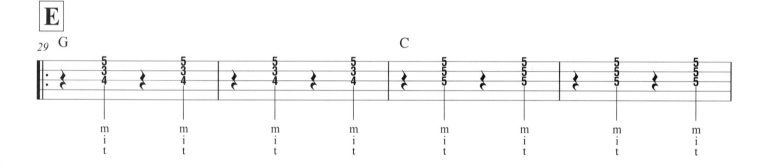

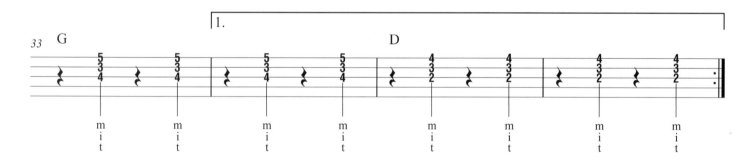

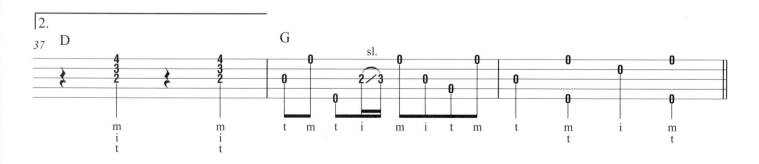

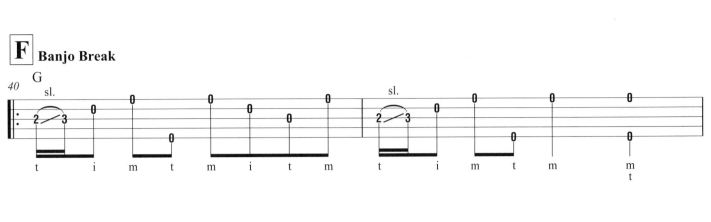

F Banjo Break

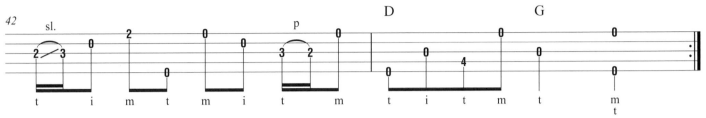

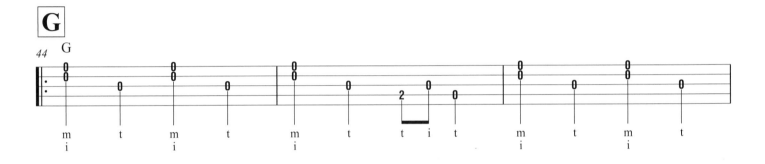

G

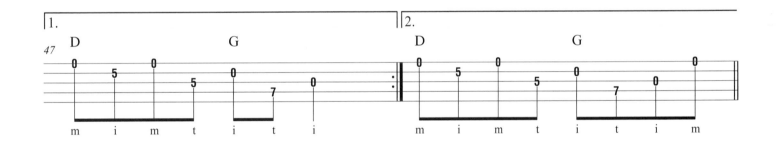

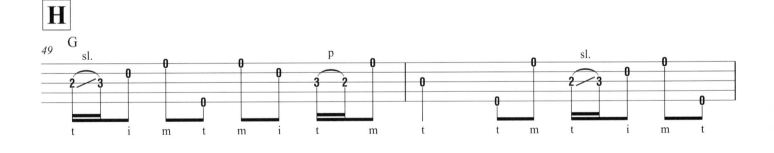

H

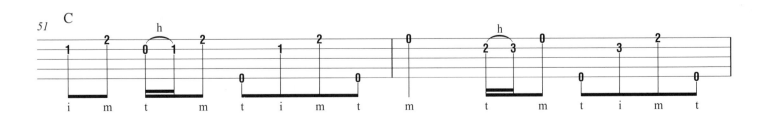

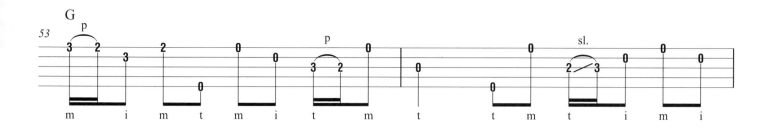

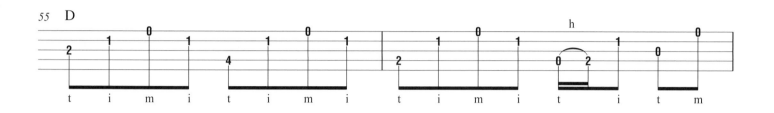

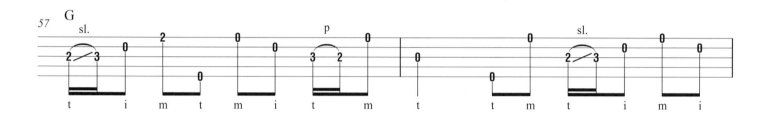

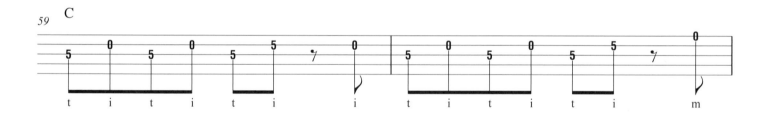

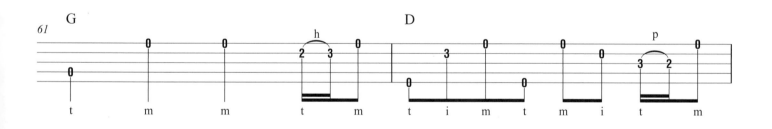

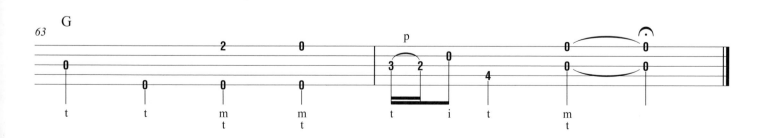

THE RED HAIRED BOY
Old Time Fiddle Tune

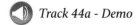 *Track 44a - Demo*

Track 44b - Play-Along

G tuning:
(5th-1st) G-D-G-B-D

Key of A
Capo II

 **Banjo Break**

Moderately slow ♩ = 94

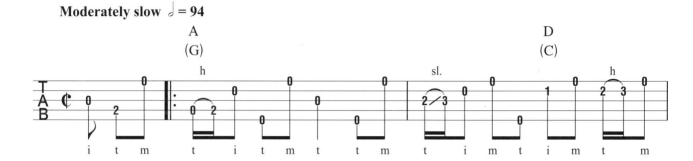

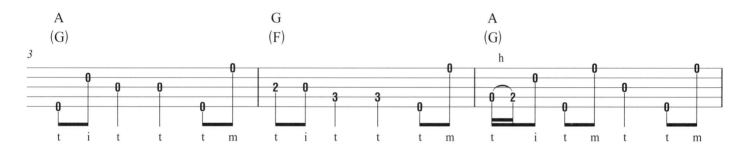

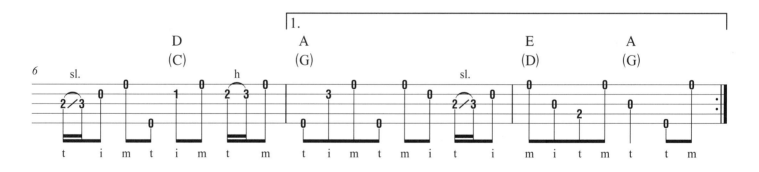

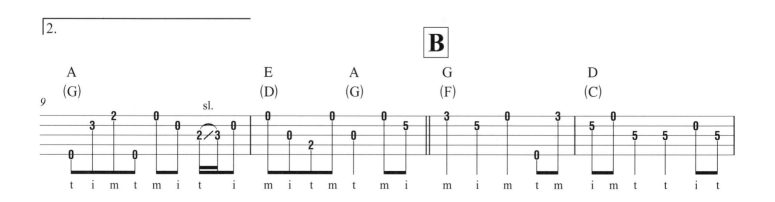

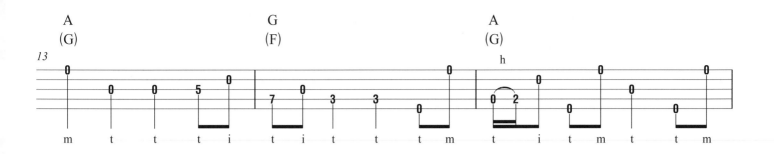

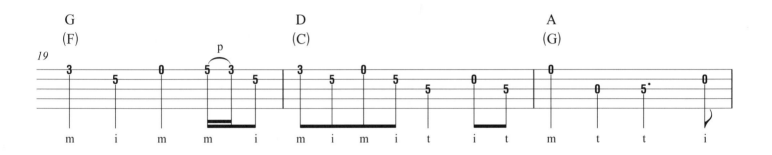

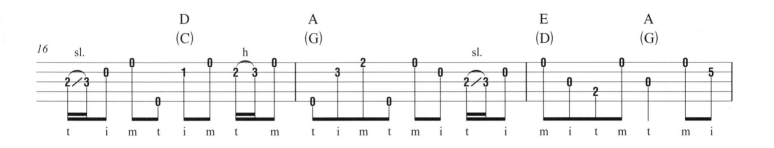

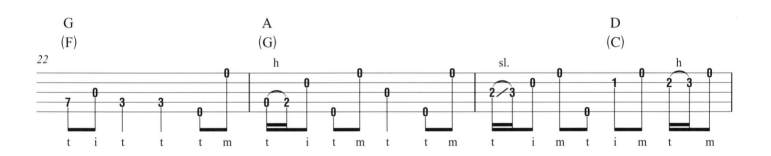

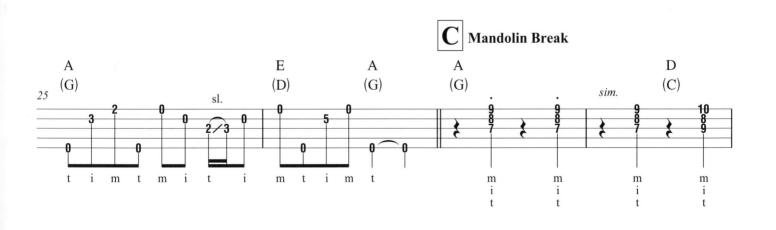

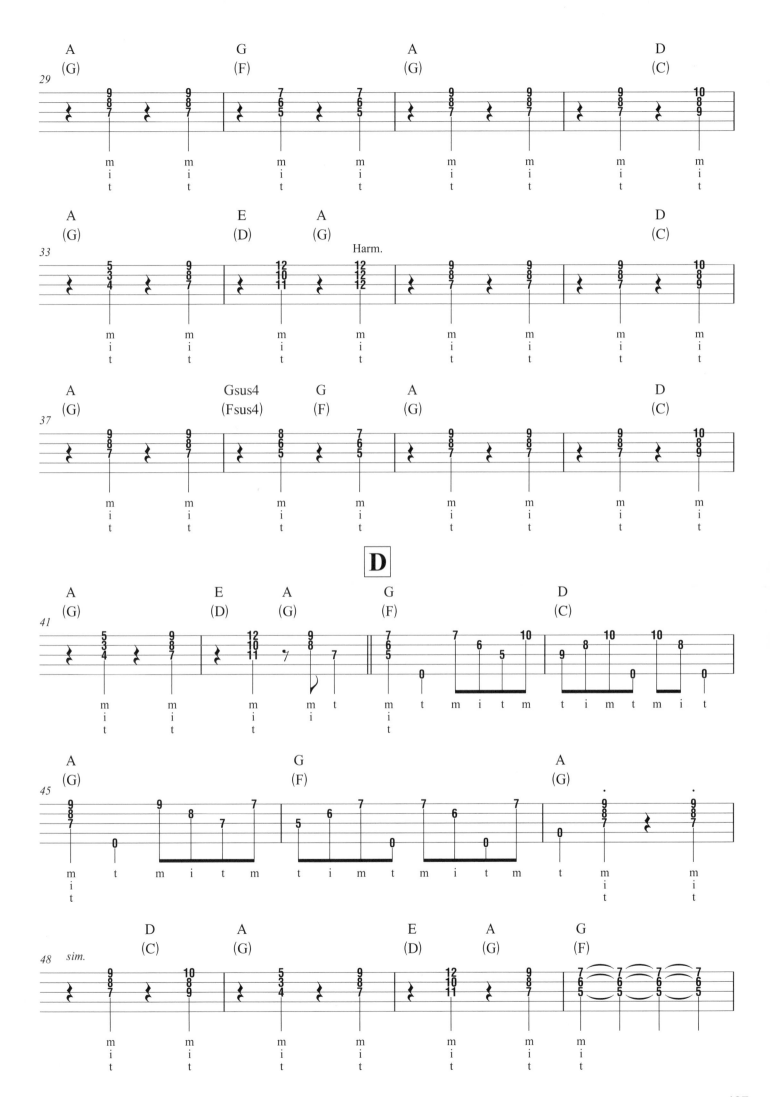

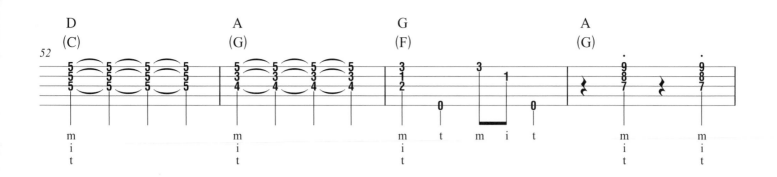

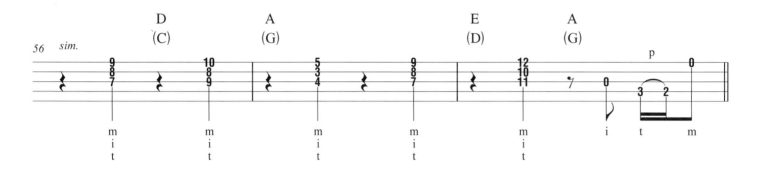

E Banjo Break

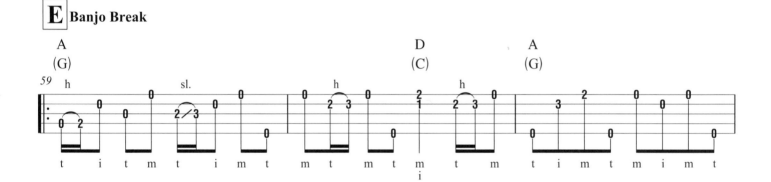

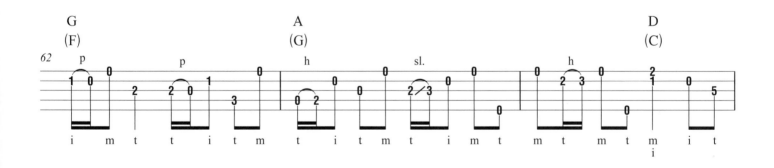

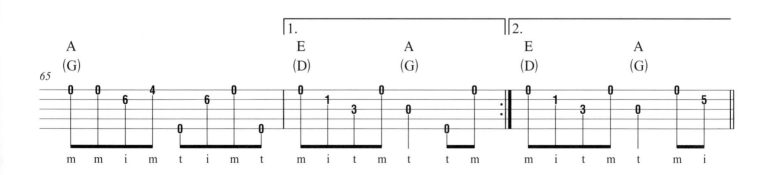

F

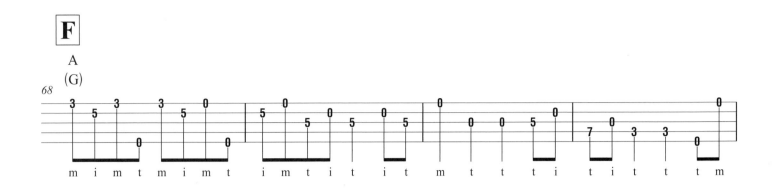

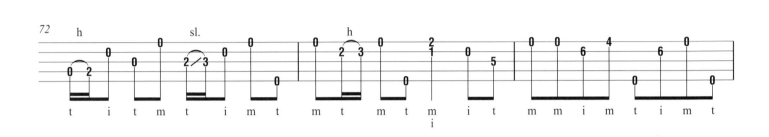

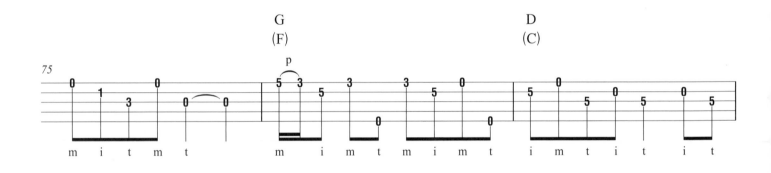

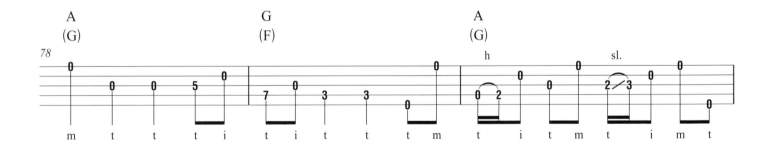

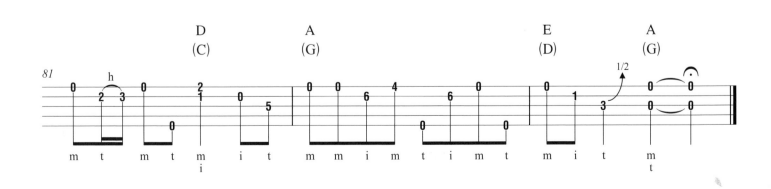

EIGHTH OF JANUARY

Traditional

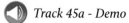 Track 45a - Demo

Track 45b - Play-Along

G tuning:
(5th-1st) G-D-G-B-D

Key of A
Capo II

A Banjo Break

Moderately slow ♩ = 96

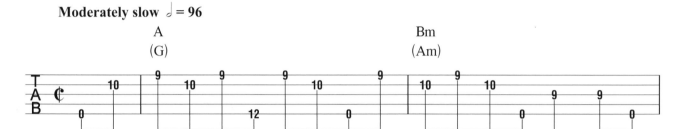

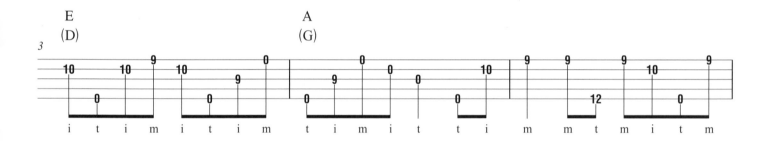

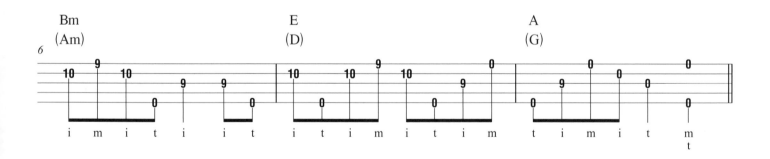

B

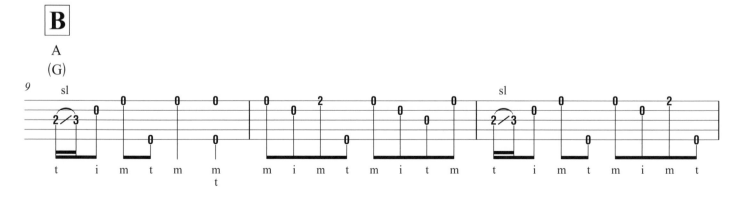

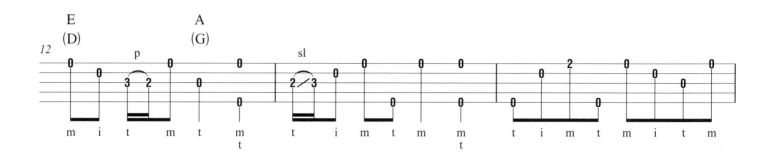

Key of D

C Mandolin Break

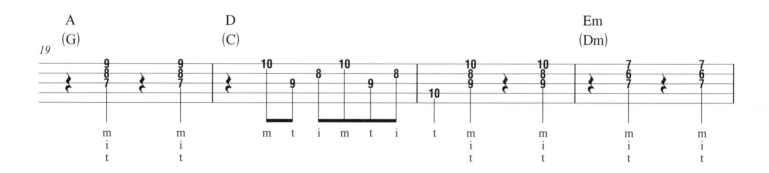

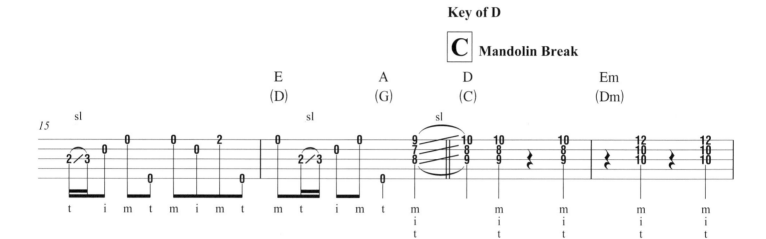

D

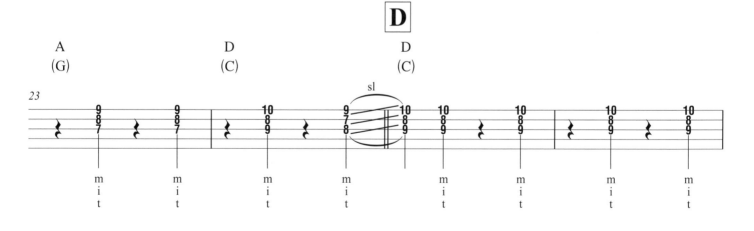

*Capo VII

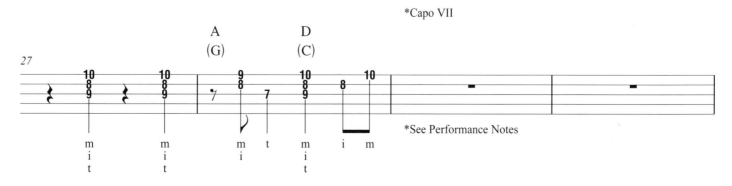

*See Performance Notes

111

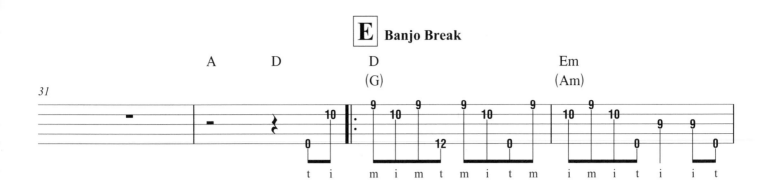

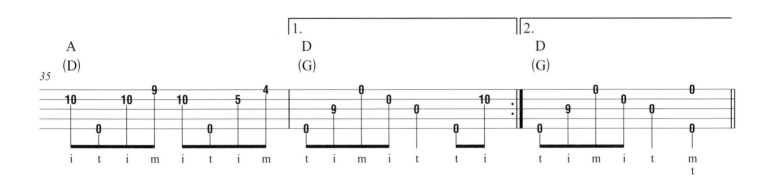

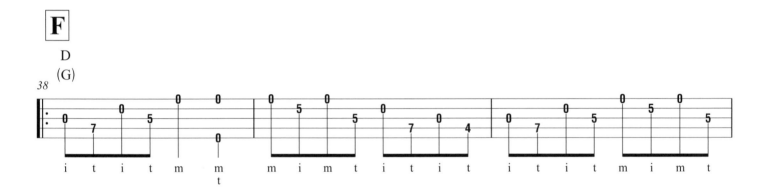

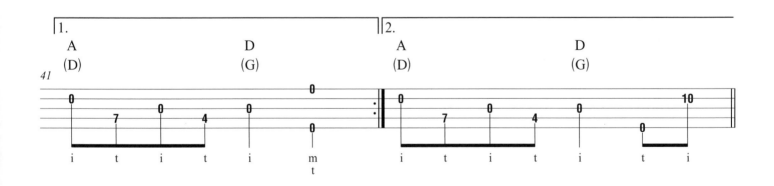

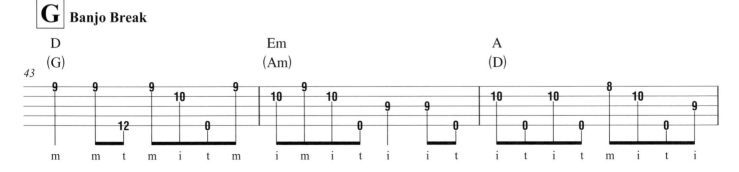

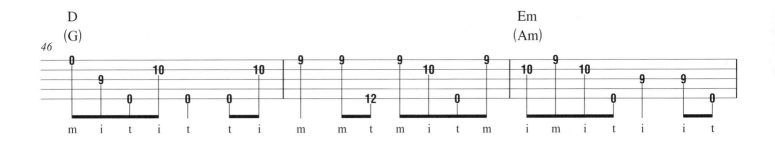

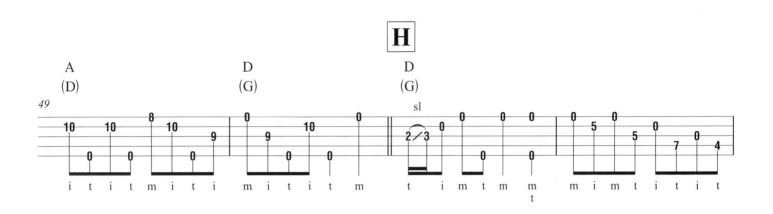

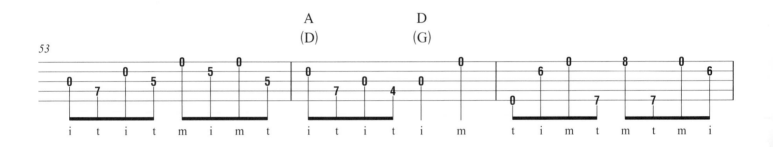

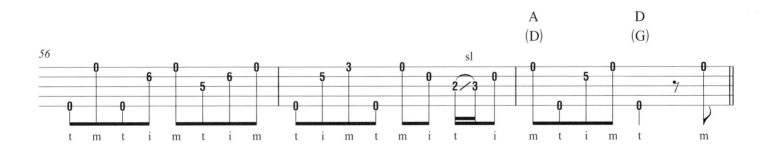

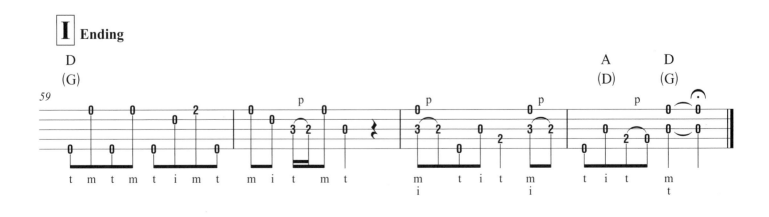

Appendix B:
Chord Glossary

This is an abbreviated chord glossary. By "abbreviated," I mean that it includes the chords you will use regularly, while omitting those that aren't commonly used in bluegrass music. When it comes time to research the less common types, there are many books out there (such as the *Hal Leonard Banjo Chord Finder*) that will list any chord you can think of, and very probably, a whole bunch that you never would have. That said, we will focus on the various forms of major, minor, and seventh chords, with commentary on how and where they might be used to their best advantage.

- The chord grids represent the fingerboard of the 5-string banjo. Horizontal lines represent the frets, while vertical lines represent the strings. Notice that the *first-position* chord grids (or those formed on the lowest frets) include a heavier vertical line at the top. This represents the nut. There are only four strings shown at the nut; the 5th string starts at the 5th fret. In other chords that are fretted on higher-numbered frets (or "up the neck"), notice that the nut is no longer shown and the grid consists of all five strings. The fret number is given so you'll know where to form the chord.

- The fingers used to fret the chords are indicated by black dots with letters inside: I, M, R, and P. These tell you where to use the index (I), middle (M), ring (R), or pinky (P) fingers for that particular chord position. In some chord grids, you might notice a dot that is not black. This is an optional fingering. For example, for any chord using the D position, the ring finger is optional. It may be needed for a melody note or a different voicing, but in many cases, it's not needed. This is particularly true when playing backup. If you're using a D-position G chord, you're probably only hitting the first two or three strings. That said, avoid the temptation to use the ring finger on the 1st string. Use the pinky as shown. That way, it will be a habit, and if you suddenly decide you need the 4th string fretted, all you have to do is reach over with the ring finger.

- Notice that some chord grids include an "X" or an "O" hovering over the top of one or more strings. An "O" over a string means you should play that string *open*, as part of the chord. An "X" indicates that the string should *not* be played with this chord. There is an exception: If you see an optional fingering dot (white background) on an "X" string, it can be played *if* that finger is down.

Types of Chords

We've discussed major and minor chords. There are three "shapes" used to create most chords. Major chords use the barre, D-position, and F-position shapes. Minor chords use the Am, Dm, and Em positions. No matter where you place one of these movable shapes on the neck, it always results in another major or minor chord. The chord's position on the neck determines the chord's note name. For instance, play a D major chord. Now, move that chord position up the neck. Wherever you place it, it will still be a major chord, but the specific frets covered will determine which chord name it is, such as an E chord, G chord, B chord, etc.

Seventh chords are special. This type of chord is usually a variation on a major chord, but there are minor seventh chords, as well. Seventh chords are used for flavor and maybe as the occasional signal or anticipation of an upcoming chord change.

Major Chords

Let's begin with the standards. You will find that the majority of bluegrass tunes use three main chords: I, IV, and V. And with that in mind, many are in the key of G, or capoed but still played as though they're in G. So, let's start with these common chords.

There are three shapes used to produce a major chord: barre, F-position, and D-position.

- The barre is produced by laying a single finger across multiple strings, all on the same fret. In the G example below, the first and fourth examples are barres (the first is open; the nut acts as the barre).

- Forming an F chord will also create a movable major chord shape. Moving this same shape to different places on the neck determines which major chord it is. For example, to play an F-position G chord, simply play it two frets above the regular F chord.

- The same goes for D position—placing that shape anywhere on the neck will produce a major chord. Here, a D-position shape with the index on the 7th fret will create a G chord. This one in particular is useful in back-up playing.

G

The standard banjo tuning of the five unfretted strings is an open G chord. "Open" means that strumming all the open strings, without any frets being used, produces a G major chord.

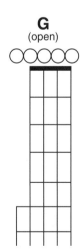

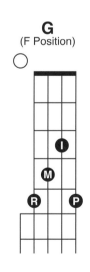

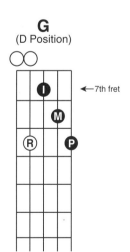

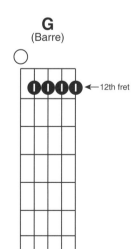

C

Notice that the fretted notes of the first C chord grid are in the same general position as a D chord, except that the 3rd string is open. But if you move the whole shape up the neck, you'd have to fret that 3rd string to maintain the chord voicing, thereby forming the complete D-position shape.

The third C grid is an F position with the index finger on the 8th fret. When playing backup, it's a good idea to find the chords closest to one another. In this case, this C is one fret above the D-position G, so when changing from I to IV (G to C), you would only have to slide up one fret and switch positions.

Notice the fourth grid here. It's just like the basic C, except that the 1st string is not fretted. This is a nice way to voice a C (use it sparingly) for a slightly different feel.

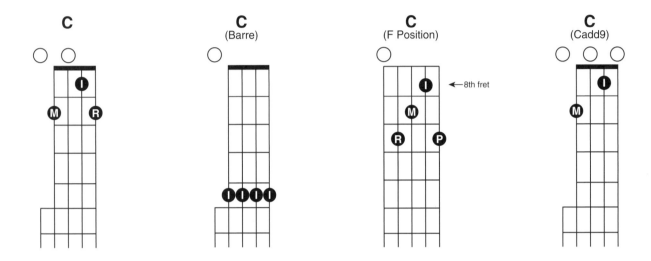

D

Every D is the same as every C grid, only two frets higher. Again, when playing backup, the F-position D chord is useful. It's the same position as the C—just slide it up two frets.

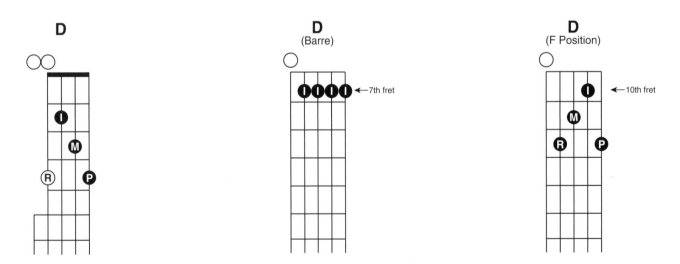

A

A
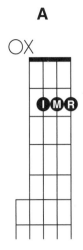

A
(Barre)
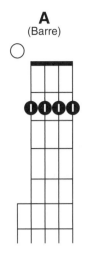

A
(F Position)
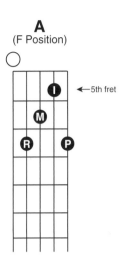
← 5th fret

A
(D Position)
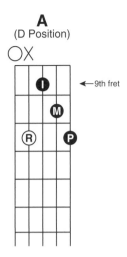
← 9th fret

B

B
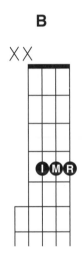

B
(Barre)
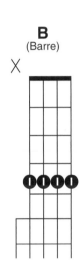

B
(F Position)
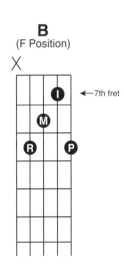
← 7th fret

B
(D Position)
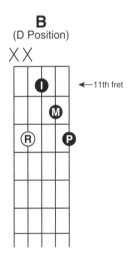
← 11th fret

E

E
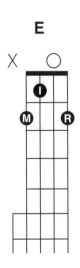

E
(D Position)
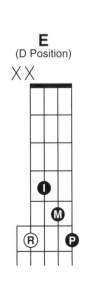

E
(Barre)
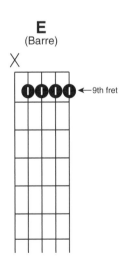
← 9th fret

E
(F Position)
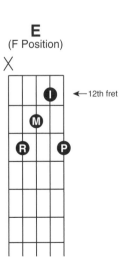
← 12th fret

117

F

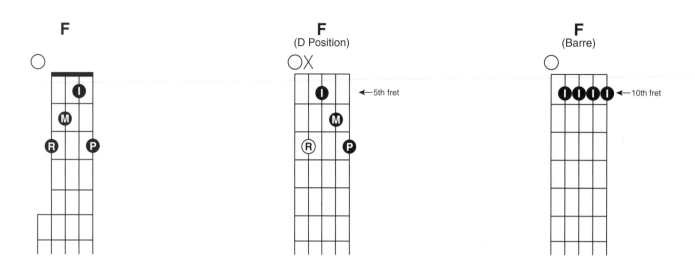

Minor Chords

Minor chords have a different feel. Earlier in the book, you learned that major chords are built with the 1st, 3rd, and 5th degrees of the corresponding major scale. For minor chords, the 3rd is a half step (or one fret) lower, just as the corresponding minor scale has a lowered 3rd. For example, if you play the basic D major chord followed by the first D minor grid in this section (Dm), notice that the note on the 1st string is one fret lower in the minor chord. The other notes are the same.

Sometimes a song in a major key will use the occasional minor chord, making for an interesting sound. Other times, the entire song will be in a minor key, using mostly (or all) minor chords. A minor chord sounds darker or more serious, so a serious ballad might be in a minor key.

Em

In many cases, a song in a major key like G will use an E minor chord here and there. Notice that the third grid here is an Am-position Em chord. Imagine you're already playing a D-position G chord. You could leave the fingering as is and just put your unused ring finger on the 9th fret of the 3rd string (without lifting any of the other fingers), and you'd have the Em. This is shown in the fourth grid.

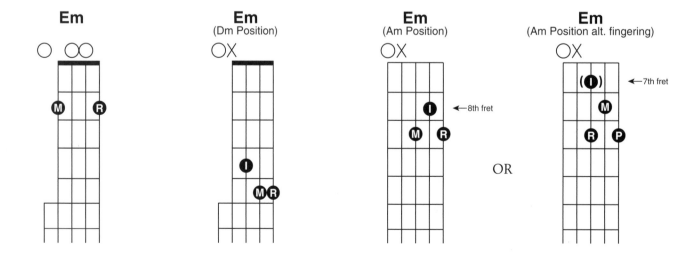

Furthermore, this position works in any key. If you're playing backup—whether chops or rolls—and you start with a D-position I chord, try the chord move below. Notice that there are no fret numbers shown. It doesn't matter. Start with the D-position I chord; staying in place, add the ring finger to create the vi chord. Then, switch to an F position and move up one fret for the IV chord. Finally, slide that position up two frets for the V chord. Wherever you start with the I chord, just follow the progression: I–vi–IV–V.

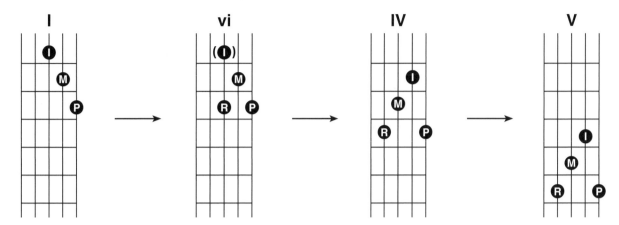

Following are some more minor chords...

Am

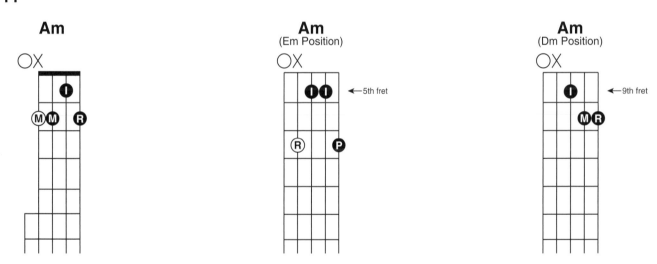

Notice the first Am grid above. Fret the 3rd string with the middle finger, and do not play the fourth string *unless* you move the middle finger over to that string.

Bm

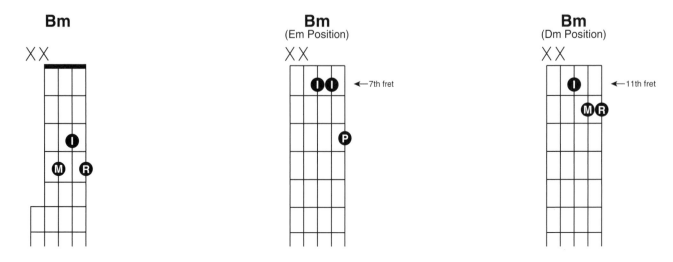

Cm

Cm
(Barre)

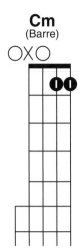

Cm
(Am Position)

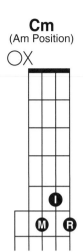

Cm
(Em Position)

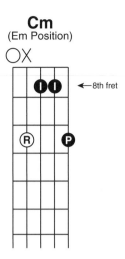
← 8th fret

Dm

Dm

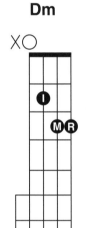

Dm
(Am Position)

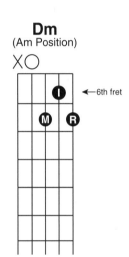
← 6th fret

Dm
(Em Position)

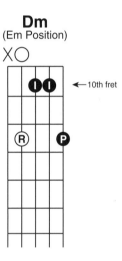
← 10th fret

Fm

Fm
(Em Position)

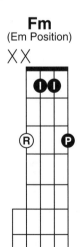

Fm
(Dm Position)

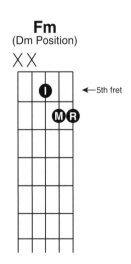
← 5th fret

Fm
(Am Position)

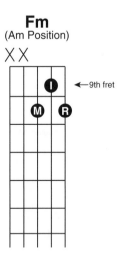
← 9th fret

Gm

Gm
(Em Position)

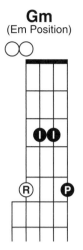

Gm
(Dm Position)

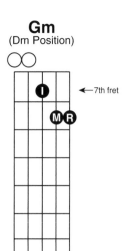
←7th fret

Gm
(Am Position)

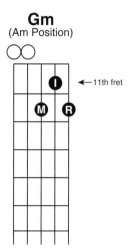
←11th fret

Seventh Chords

The seventh chord is most often used as an option to signal or anticipate a certain type of chord change. For example, you might be playing along on a G chord when a brief G7 chord appears, signaling that there's a C chord change coming up. This is handy for other players, but it also just sounds nice. Thinking up a 4th from any given chord and using the seventh voicing will work: G7 to C, D7 to G, C7 to F, etc.

Note that some of these chords may be a bit difficult, especially on the lower frets where they are spaced farther apart. These might be saved for higher up the neck.

A7

A7

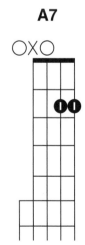

A7

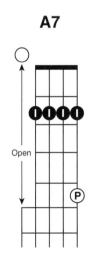
Open

A7

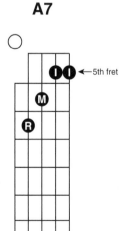
←5th fret

A7

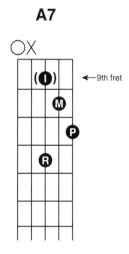
←9th fret

Notice in the second grid of A7 we have an option to play either the 1st string, 5th fret *or* the 5th string open. It's the same note, so if you're playing a roll, it's probably easier to just use the open 5th string.

B7

B7
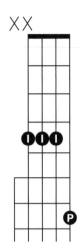

B7
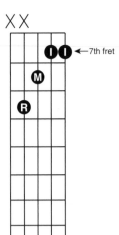
← 7th fret

B7
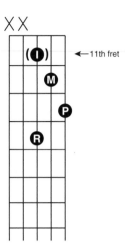
← 11th fret

C7

C7
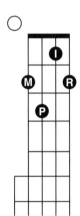

C7
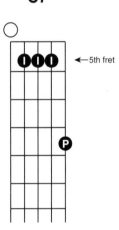
← 5th fret

C7
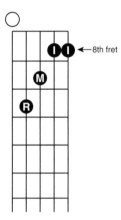
← 8th fret

D7

D7
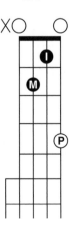

D7
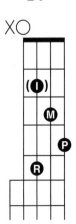

D7
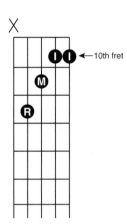
← 10th fret

E7

E7
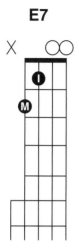

E7
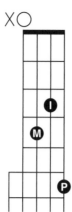

E7
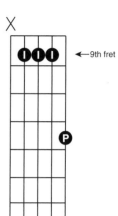

← 9th fret

F7

F7
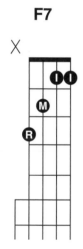

F7
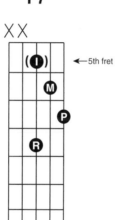

← 5th fret

F7
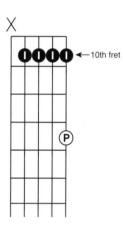

← 10th fret

G7

G7
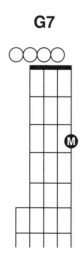

G7
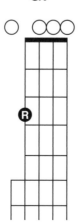

G7
(F Position)
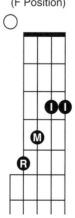

G7
(D Position)
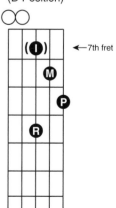

← 7th fret

BANJO NOTATION LEGEND

TABLATURE graphically represents the banjo fingerboard. Each horizontal line represents a string, and each number represents a fret.

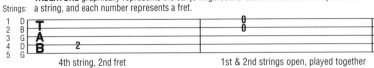

4th string, 2nd fret   1st & 2nd strings open, played together

TIME SIGNATURE:
The upper number indicates the number of beats per measure, the lower number indicates that a quarter note gets one beat.

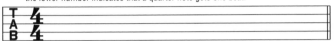

CUT TIME:
Each note's time value should be cut in half. As a result, the music will be played twice as fast as it is written.

QUARTER NOTE:
time value = 1 beat

EIGHTH NOTES:
time value = 1/2 beat each

single   in series

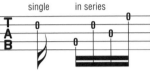

SIXTEENTH NOTES:
time value = 1/4 beat each

single   in series

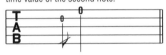

DOTTED QUARTER NOTE:
time value = 1 1/2 beat

TIE: Pick the 1st note only, then let it sustain for the combined time value.

TRIPLET: Three notes played in the same time normally occupied by two notes of the same time value.

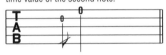
_3_

GRACE NOTE: A quickly played note with no time value of its own. The grace note and the note following it only occupy the time value of the second note.

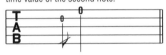

RITARD: A gradual slowing of the tempo or speed of the song.

rit.

QUARTER REST:
time value = 1 beat of silence

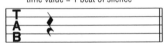

EIGHTH REST:
time value = 1/2 beat of silence

HALF REST:
time value = 2 beats of silence

WHOLE REST:
time value = 4 beats of silence

ENDINGS: When a repeated section has a first and second ending, play the first ending only the first time and play the second ending only the second time.

REPEAT SIGNS: Play the music between the repeat signs two times.

D.S. AL CODA:
Play through the music until you complete the measure labeled _"D.S. al Coda,"_ then go back to the sign (𝄋). Then play until you complete the measure labeled _"To Coda ⊕,"_ then skip to the section labeled _"⊕ Coda."_

𝄋   _To Coda ⊕_   _D.S. al Coda_   ⊕ _Coda_

HAMMER-ON: Strike the first (lower) note with one finger, then sound the higher note (on the same string) with another finger by fretting it without picking.

h

PULL-OFF: Place both fingers on the notes to be sounded. Strike the first note and without picking, pull the finger off to sound the second (lower) note.

p

SLIDE UP: Strike the first note and then slide the same fret-hand finger up to the second note. The second note is not struck.

s
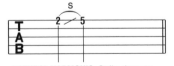

SLIDE DOWN: Strike the first note and then slide the same fret-hand finger down to the second note. The second note is not struck.

s

HALF-STEP CHOKE: Strike the note and bend the string up 1/2 step.

1/2
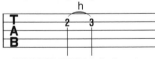

WHOLE-STEP CHOKE: Strike the note and bend the string up one step.

1

NATURAL HARMONIC: Strike the note while the fret-hand lightly touches the string directly over the fret indicated.

Harm.
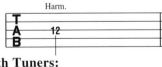

BRUSH: Play the notes of the chord indicated by quickly rolling them from bottom to top.

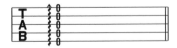

Scruggs/Keith Tuners:

HALF-TWIST UP: Strike the note, twist tuner up 1/2 step, and continue playing.

1/2
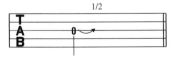

HALF-TWIST DOWN: Strike the note, twist tuner down 1/2 step, and continue playing.

1/2

WHOLE-TWIST UP: Strike the note, twist tuner up one step, and continue playing.

1

WHOLE-TWIST DOWN: Strike the note, twist tuner down one step, and continue playing.

1
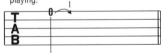

Right Hand Fingerings

t = thumb   i = index finger   m = middle finger

The End

In closing, I hope you have enjoyed this book and, more importantly, I hope you've learned a lot and it has helped you on your way to becoming a good banjo player. There are few things I find more enjoyable and rewarding than working out a new idea, technique, or tune and having one or more "aha moments" when things all come together.

Bluegrass banjo might be a casual interest for you, or it might be a passion. Either way, I hope this book has taught and demonstrated everything needed to help you become a proficient banjo player and musician.

Listen to and appreciate all music. You never know where inspiration might come from. I have gotten ideas from other bluegrass musicians, obviously, but also from classical music, rock 'n' roll, country, and even barbershop quartets. All music is great if it's done well, so open yourself up to it.

About the Author

As for myself, I've been musical as far back as I can remember. Both of my parents were very musical, so there was always music in the house.

When I was about three years old, my parents purchased a Hammond organ. My mother was a very good organist and had a great ear. I started playing it as soon as I could sit on the bench and reach the keys; and she was always there to help and make suggestions. I learned by ear and developed my musical ear while doing so.

At about the age of four, I found that if I slowed down an LP of the original early '60s Alvin and the Chipmunks, I could hear the singing—in real time—of the performer, David Seville. His three-part harmony was amazing. Then, the Beatles happened—more great three-part harmony! To this day, they are still influencing me musically.

Of course, there was band in grade school where I started on cornet (finally learning to read music). In junior high, my band director suggested that I switch to French horn. I did, and it became my major instrument in college.

I have taught middle school band and given thousands of private lessons on all band instruments, banjo, guitar, electric bass, and even the mountain dulcimer. I worked as a session musician in Nashville, TN, and as a recording engineer at Vanderbilt University. I was also a classical music DJ for the National Public Radio affiliate in Memphis, TN.

I've played banjo, guitar, and bass in several bands over the years and now run my own recording studio in South Central Wisconsin.

I have written several other books for Hal Leonard. Most of these are collections of songs in particular genres, but all are for 5-string banjo. These include bluegrass standards, Christmas songs, country songs, jam grass, and more. These are in the Banjo Play-Along series and include recordings of all the songs as a band. Each song appears twice—once with banjo so you can hear how it sounds, and once without (but with the rest of the band) so you can play along.

Acknowledgments

I would like to thank my wife, Lori Schmidt, for acting as my Tape Op and Camera Person on the video recordings, and for her wonderful vocal talents on "Think of What You've Done." I would also like to thank the Shubb Capo and Deering Banjo companies for the use of their photographs in this book.

I would also like to thank my editors, Kurt Plahna and Burgess Speed, for their experience, availability, suggestions, willingness to help, and most of all, their patience. Finally, I'd like to thank Jim Schustedt for years of patient editing, helpful suggestions, and for thinking of me when it came time to do this project.